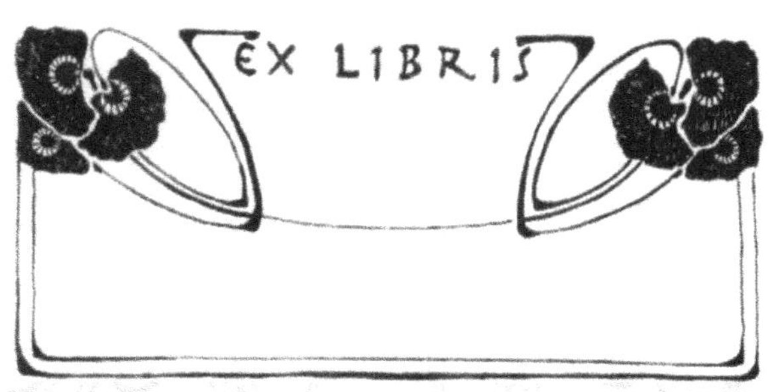

for the

entire

Color Club

BABA'S COLOR CLUB

———

My heartfelt thanks to the members of the Asheville ColorClub, from whom I got inspiration, and a great name for this book. I began making mandala/kaleidoscopes because they please my eye. All of these begin as hand-drawn pen and ink originals.

It was great meditative fun to create these, and I hope you have great meditative fun coloring them.

Many of these designs are quite detailed and intricate. There are some real surprises in the last section of this book. **Bring your best game !!**

NOTE: to keep costs down, I used normal paper. If using pens, please place a scrap sheet beneath the page to prevent ink bleed-through to the next piece of art.

---

best wishes to all

Karl Moeller
Asheville NC
2019

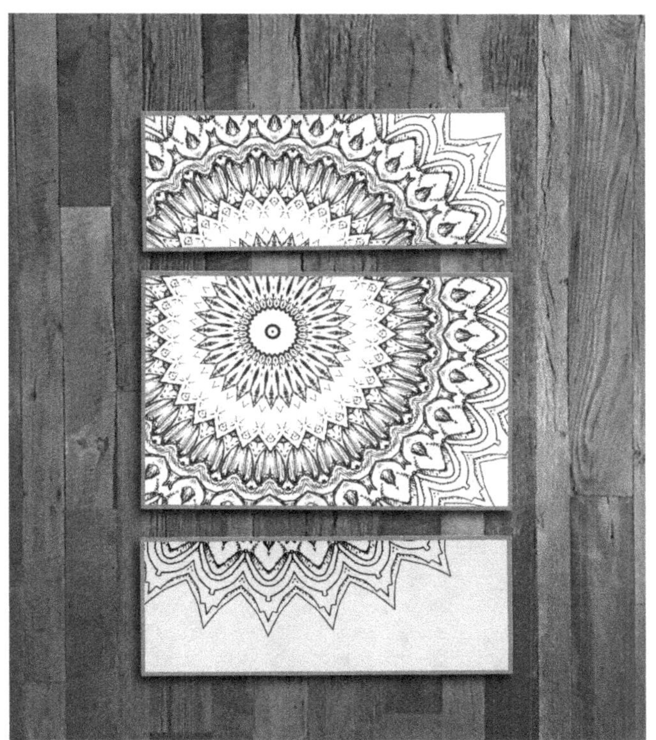

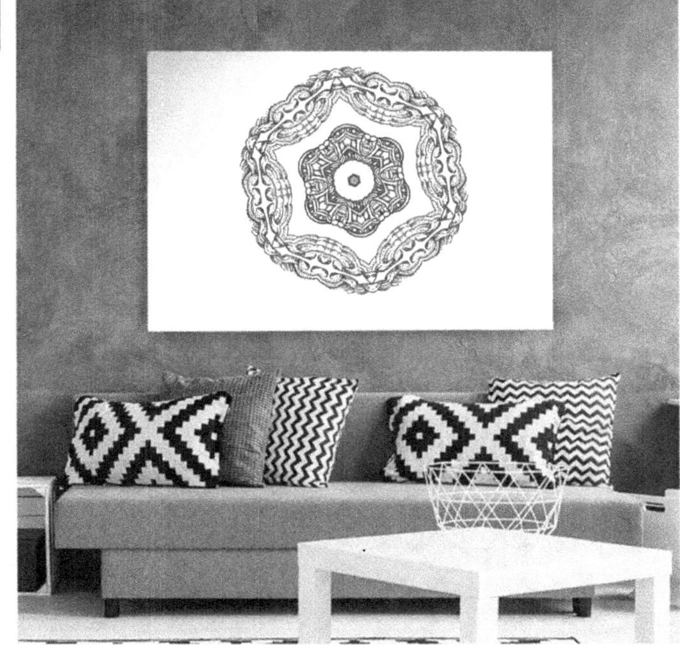

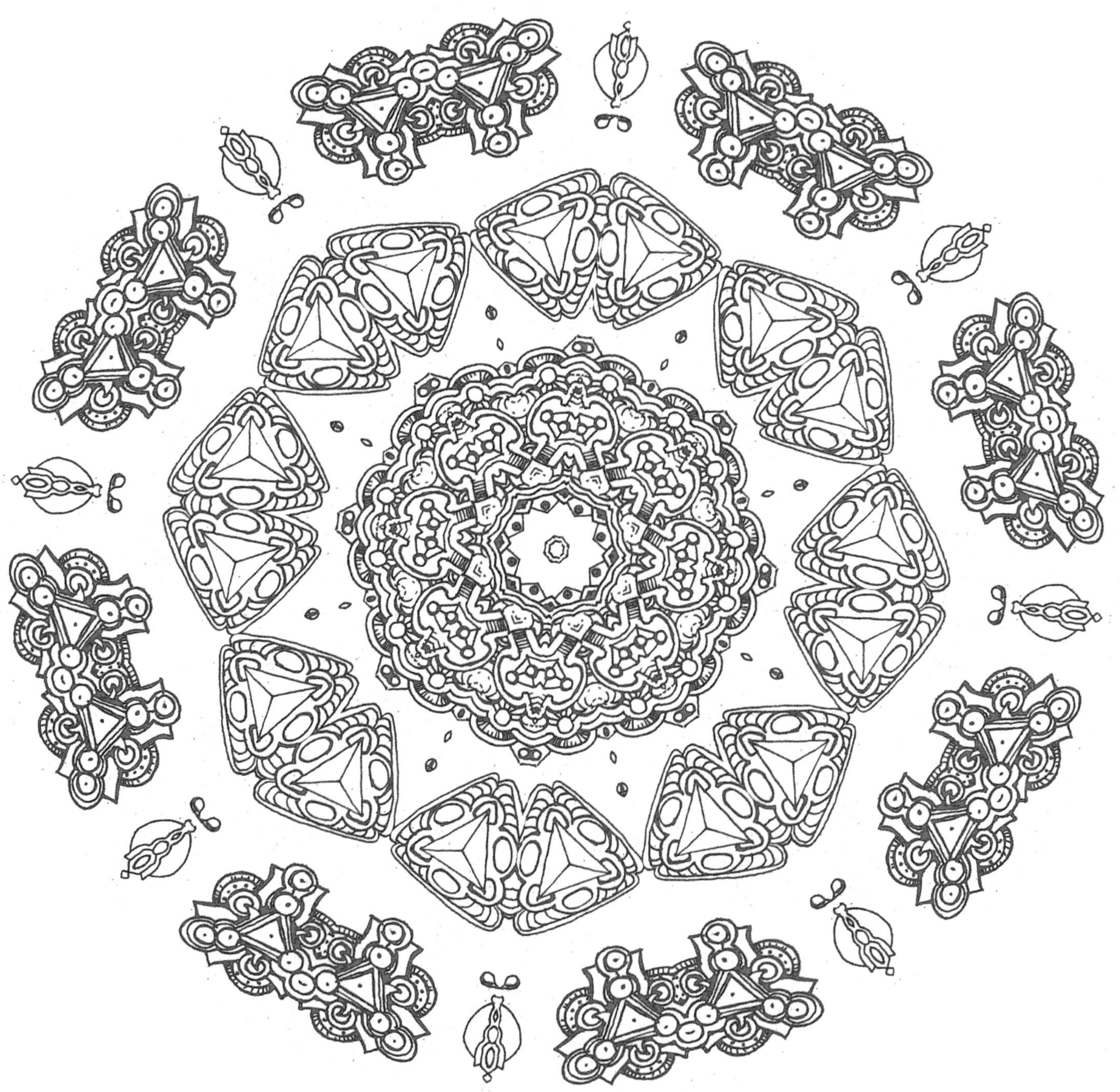

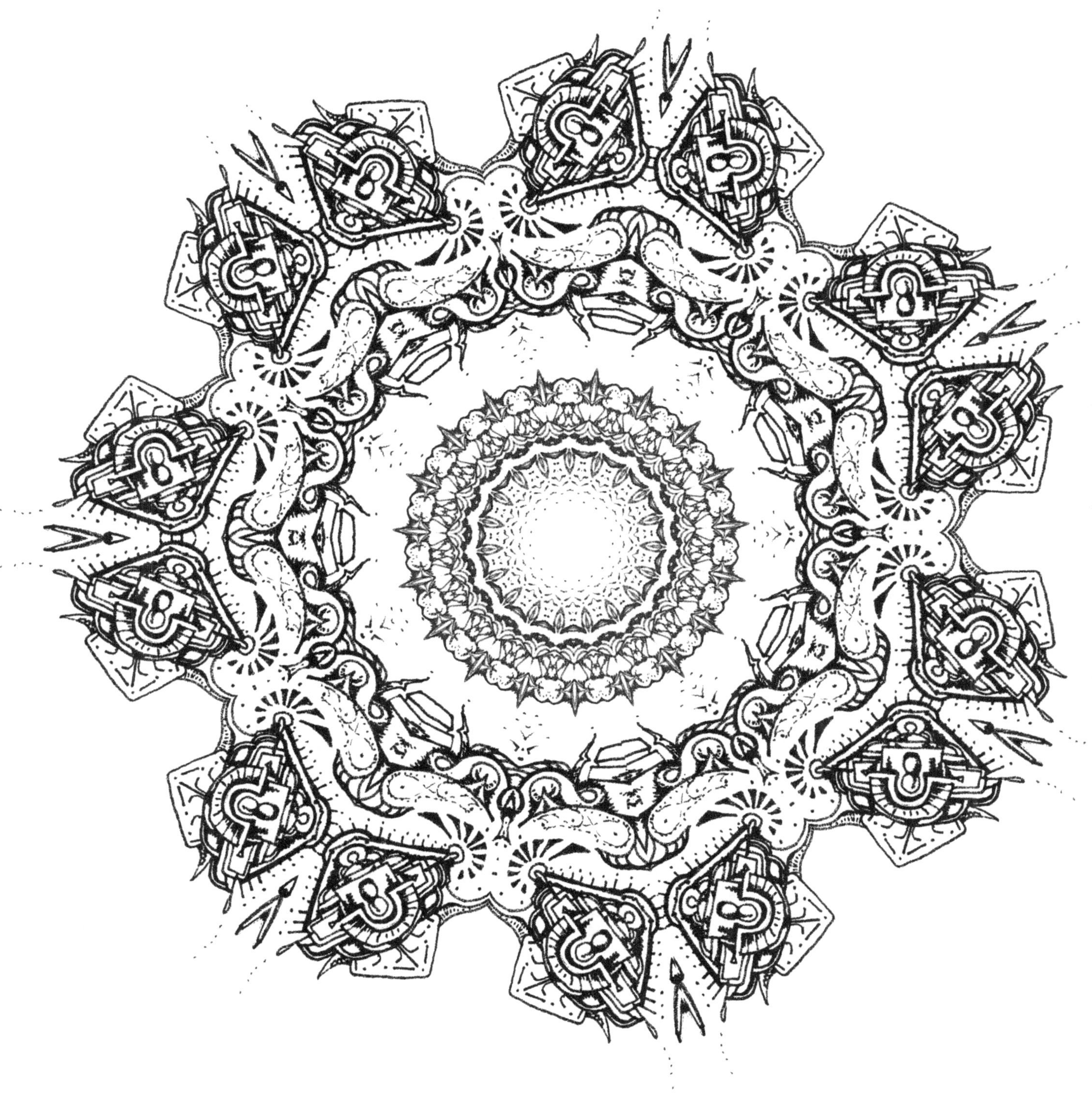

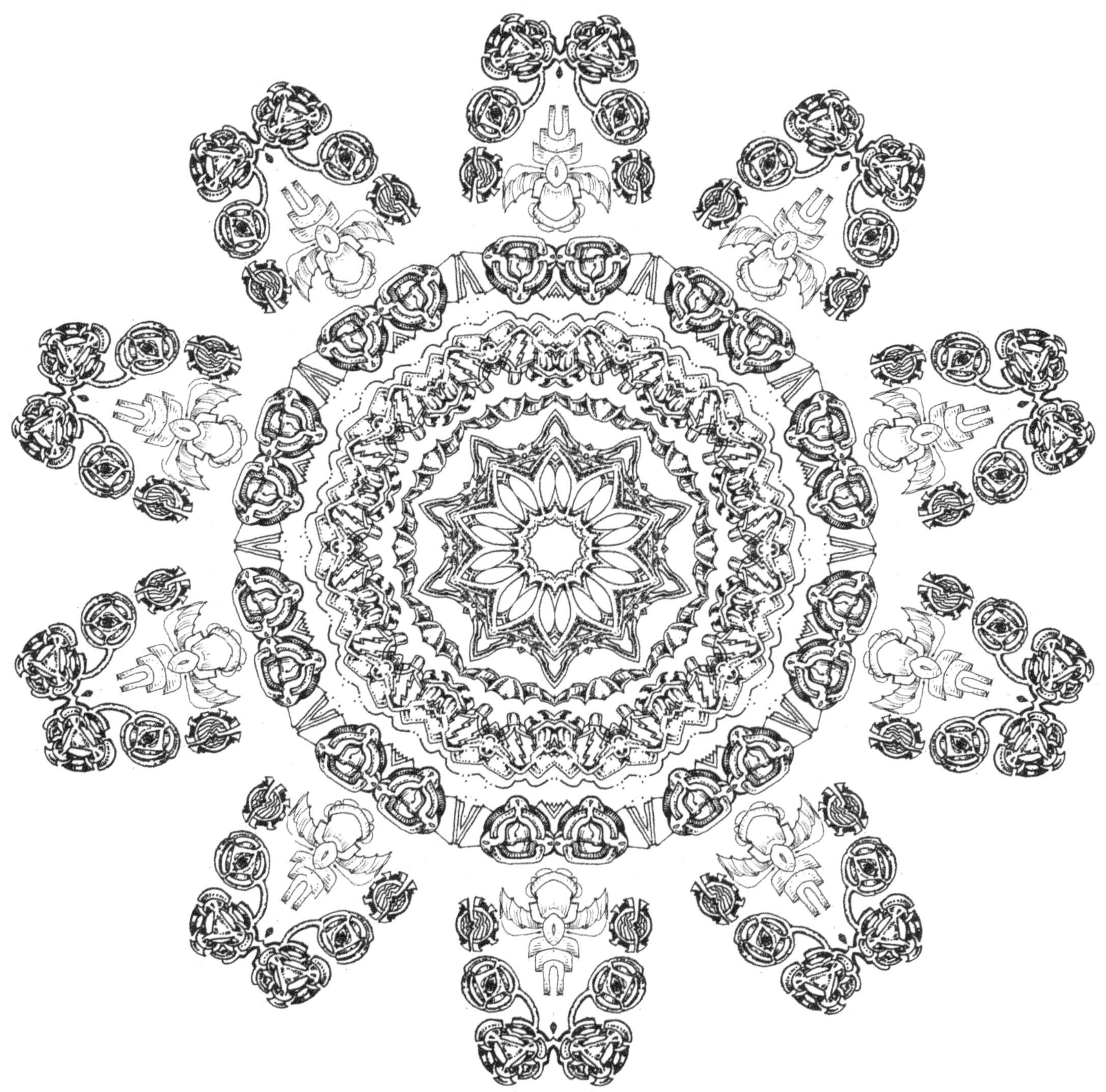

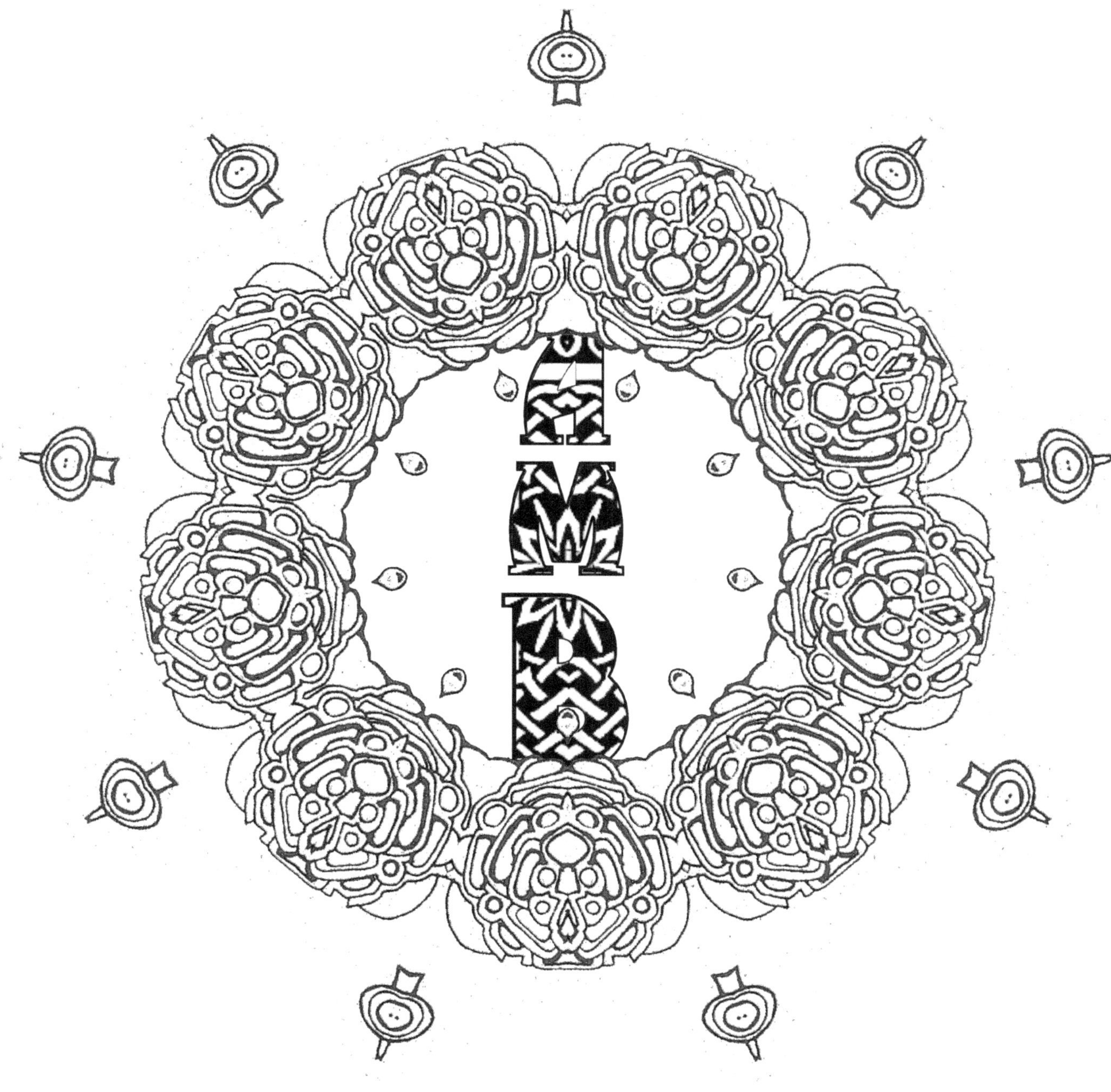

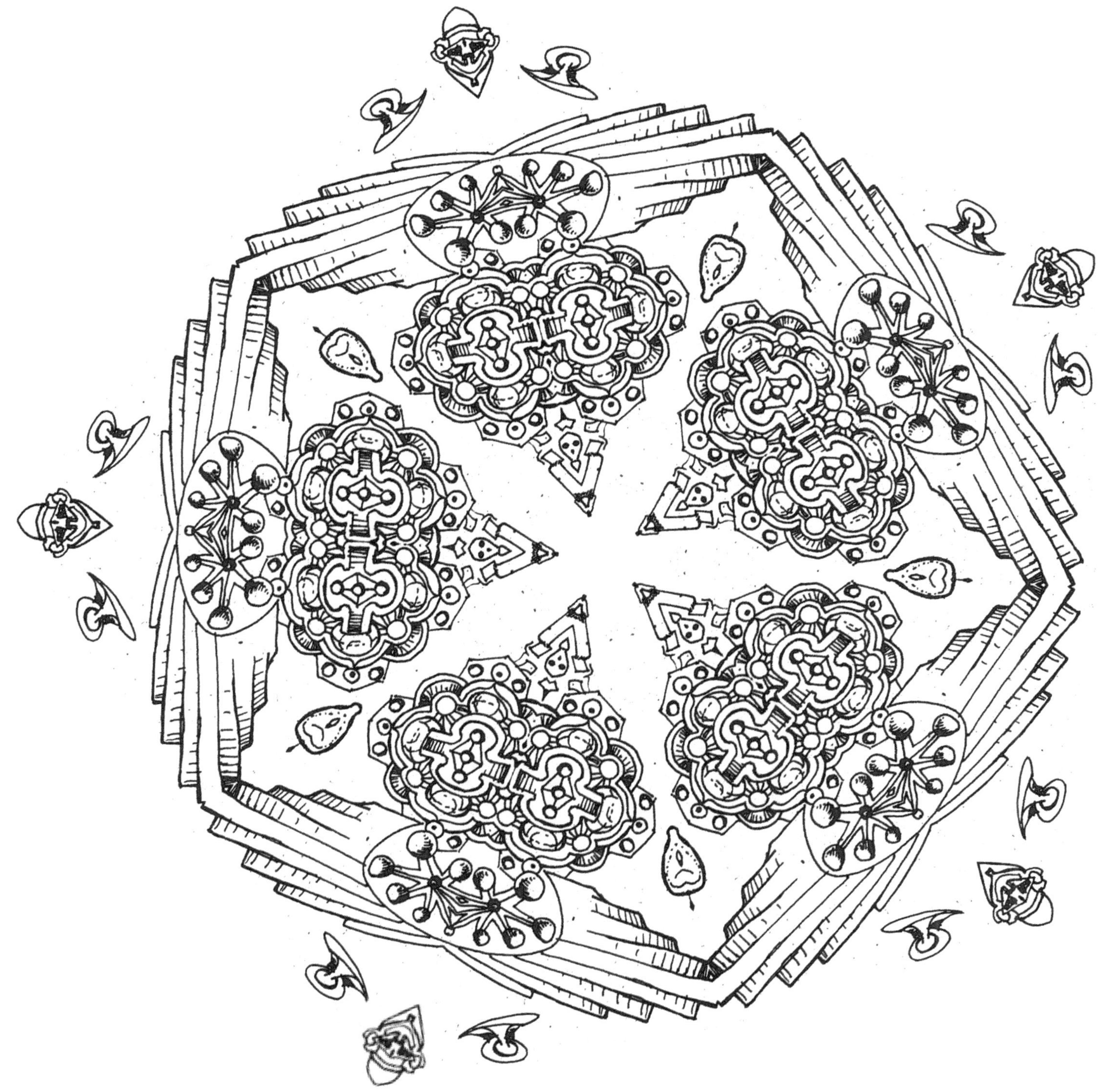

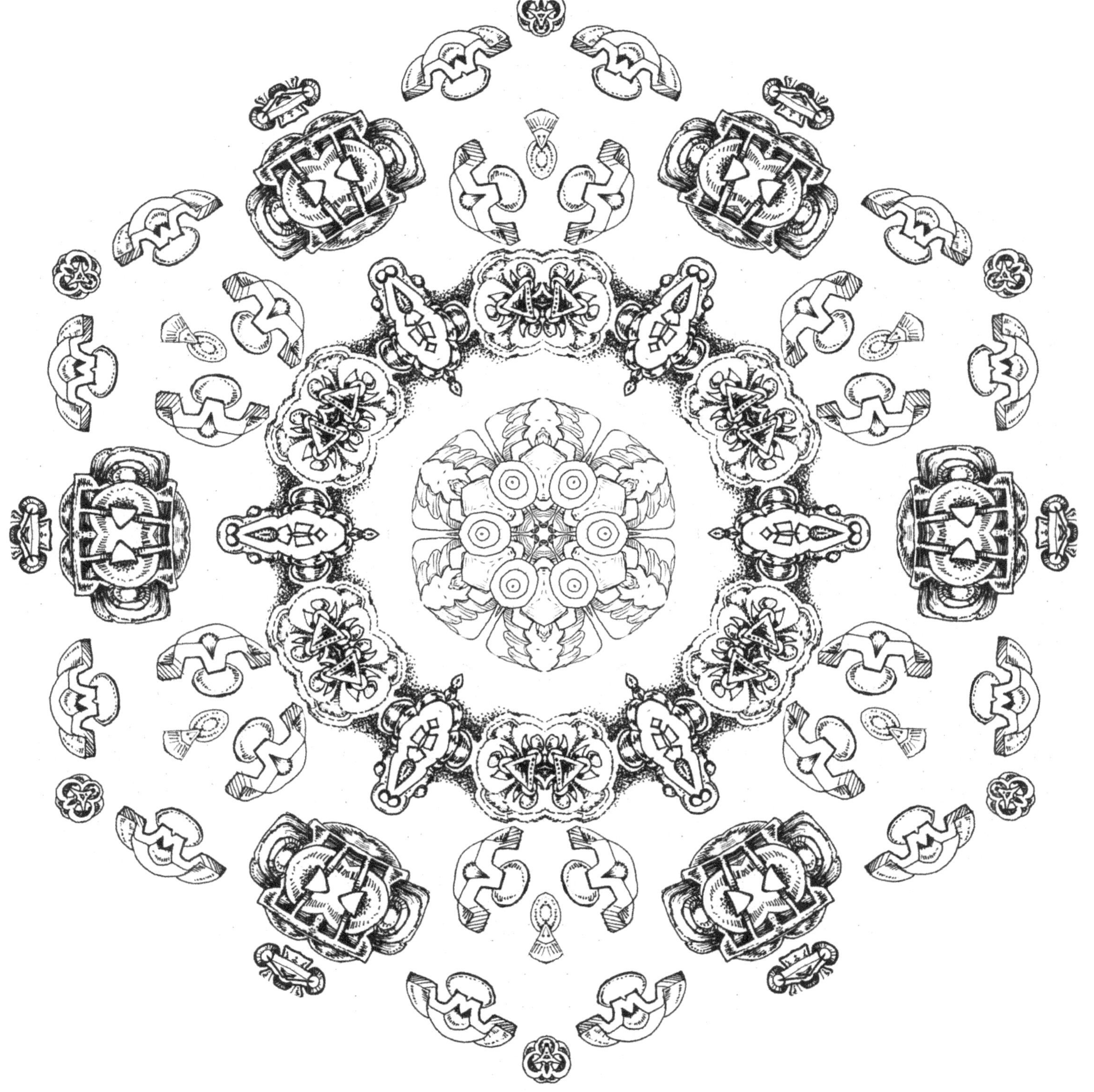

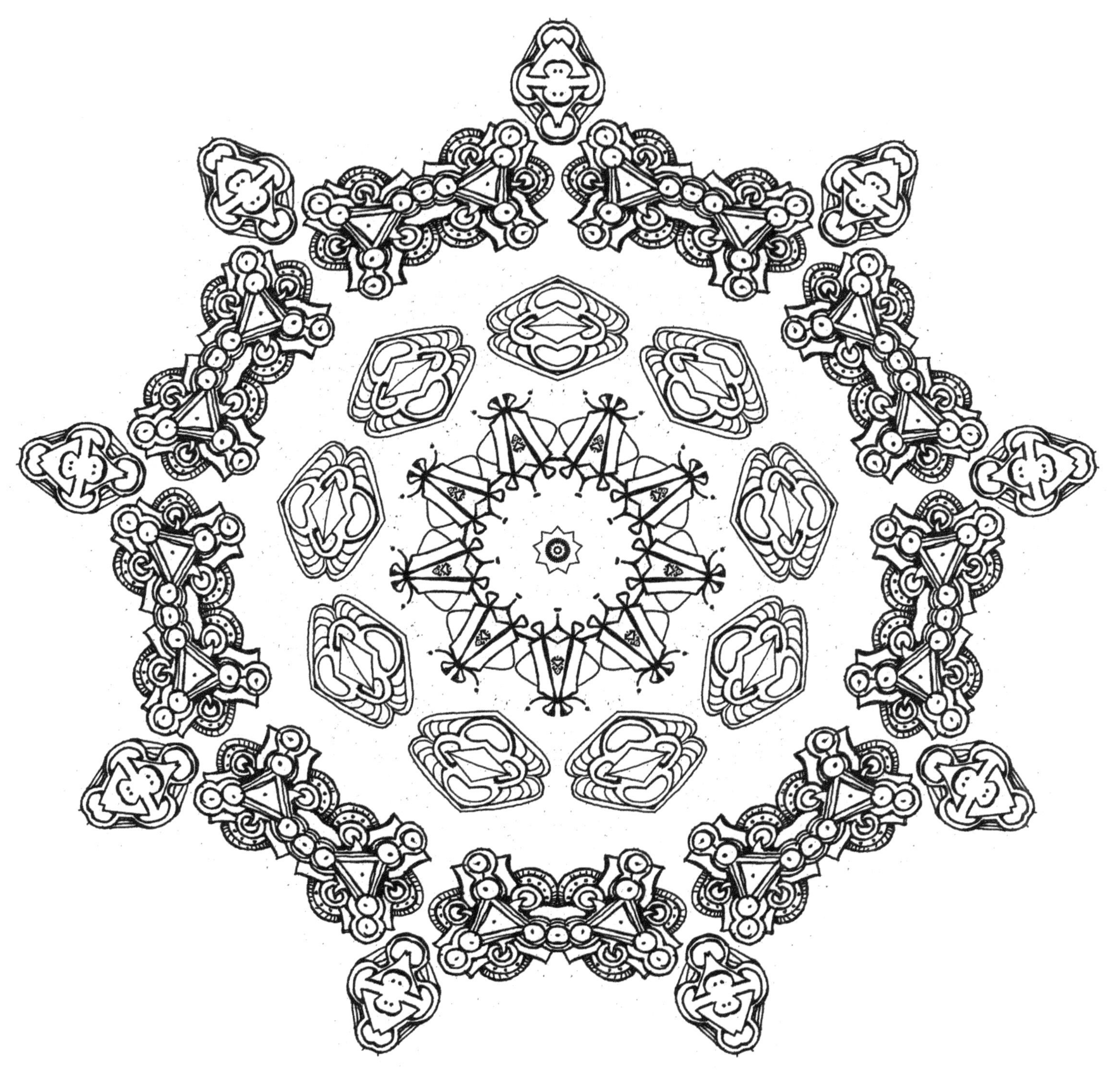

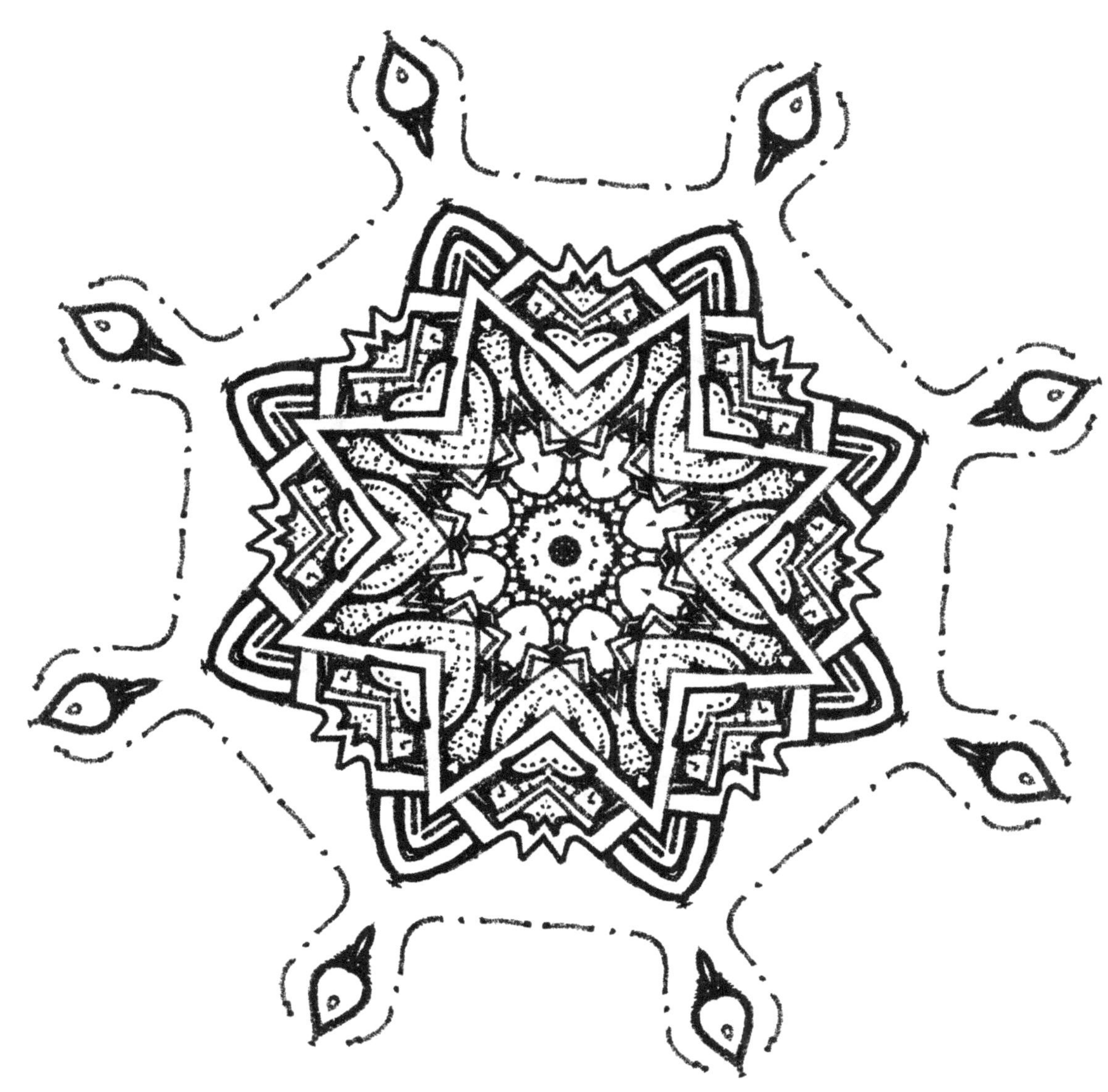

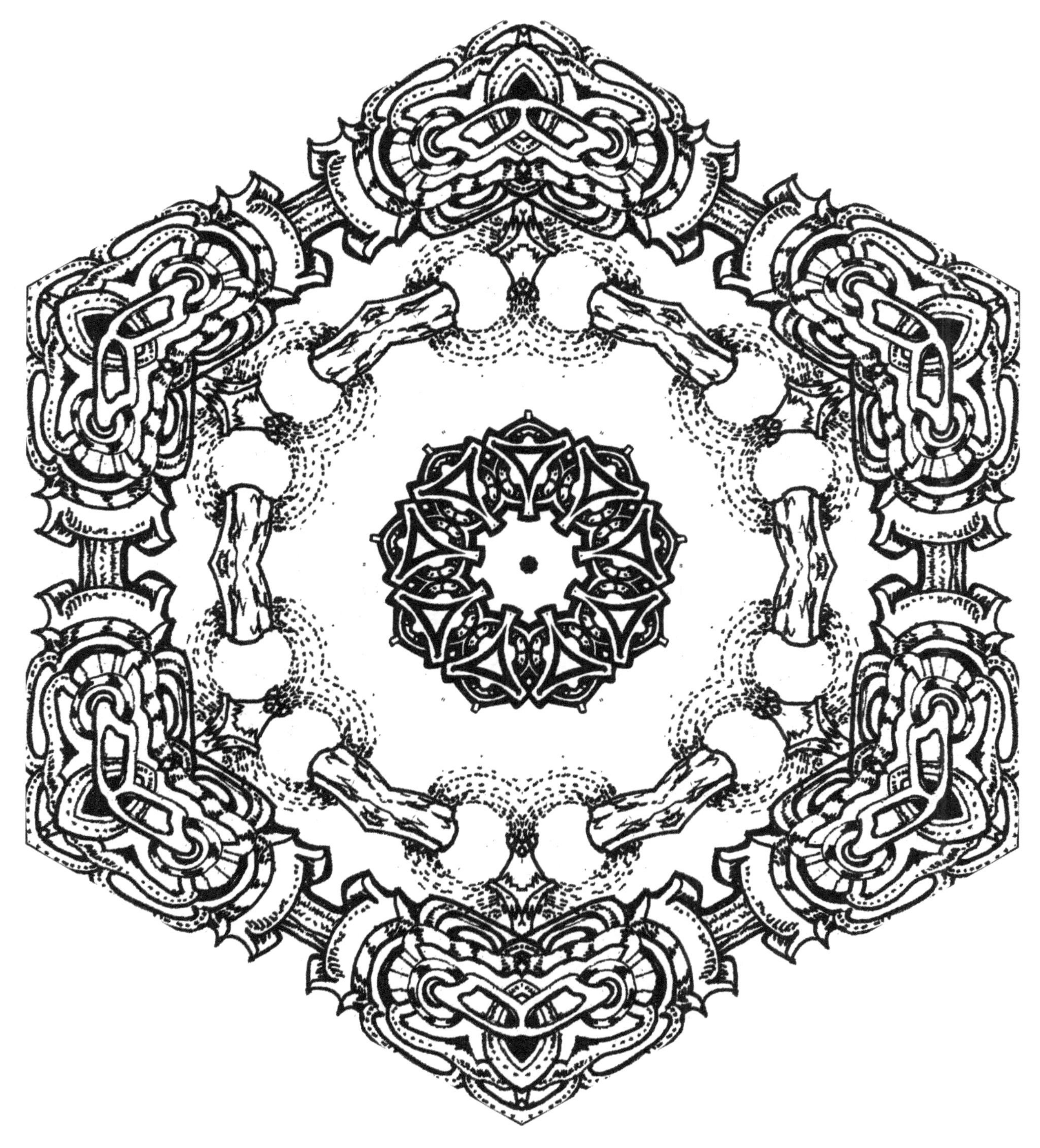

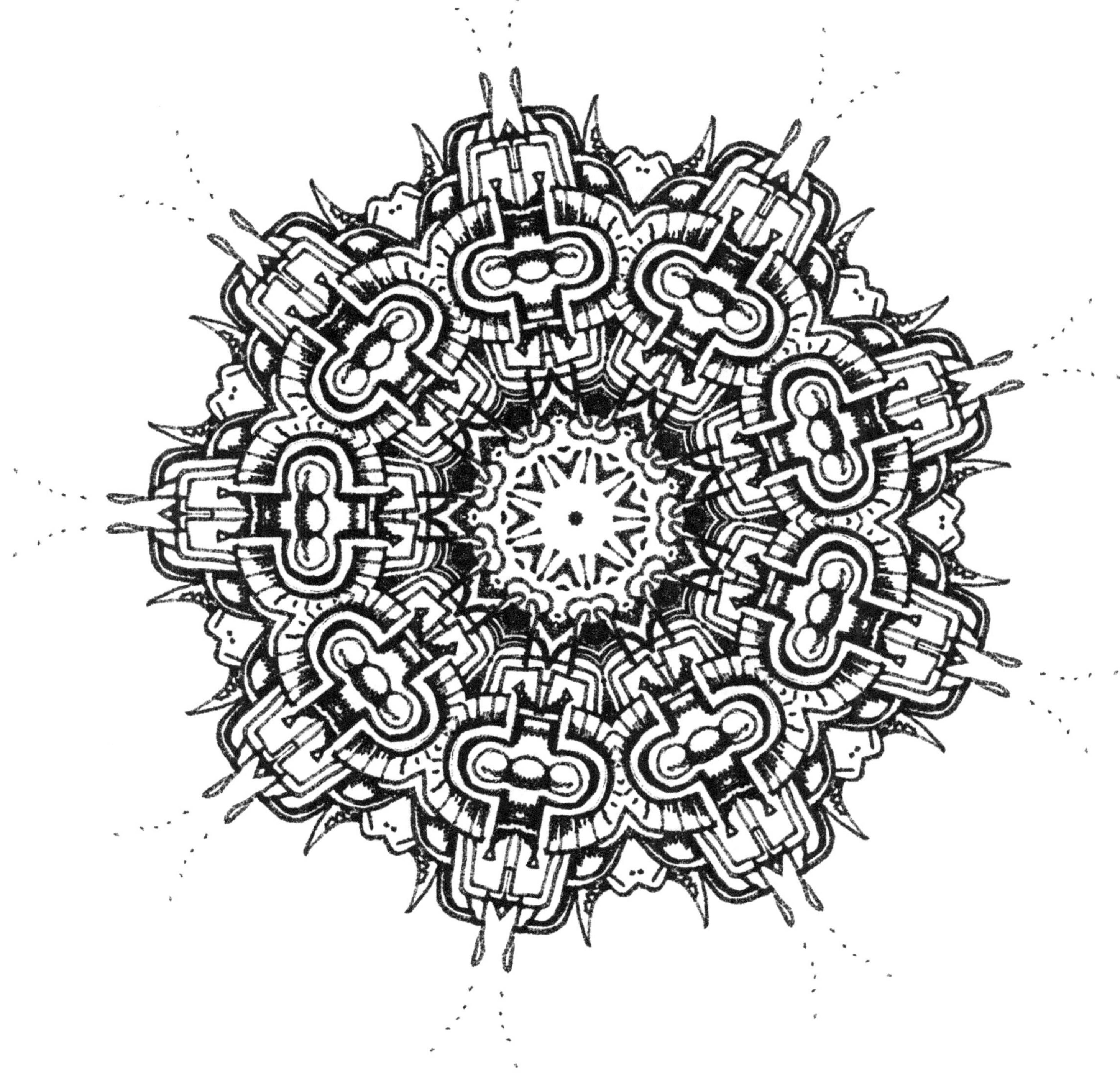

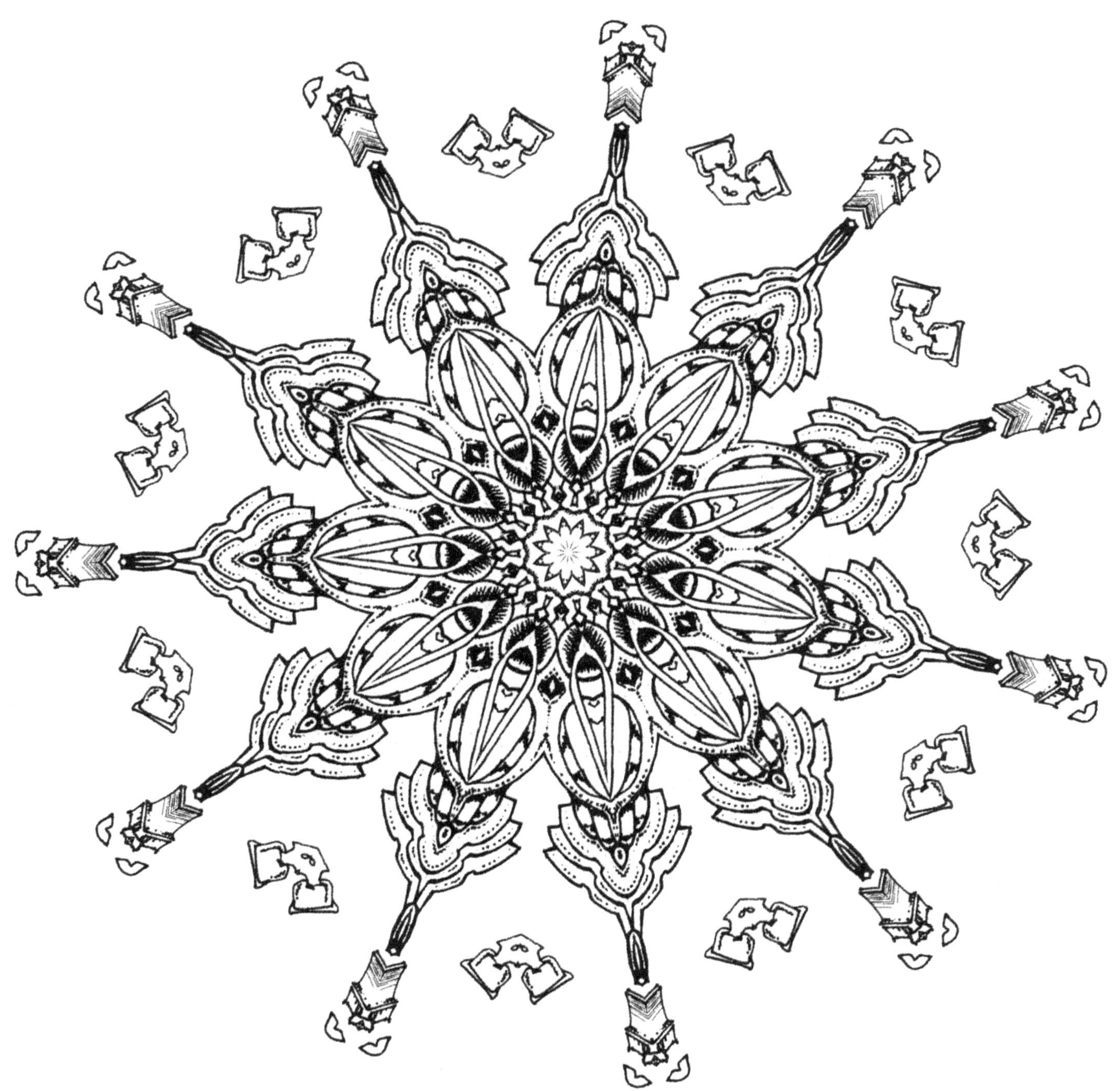

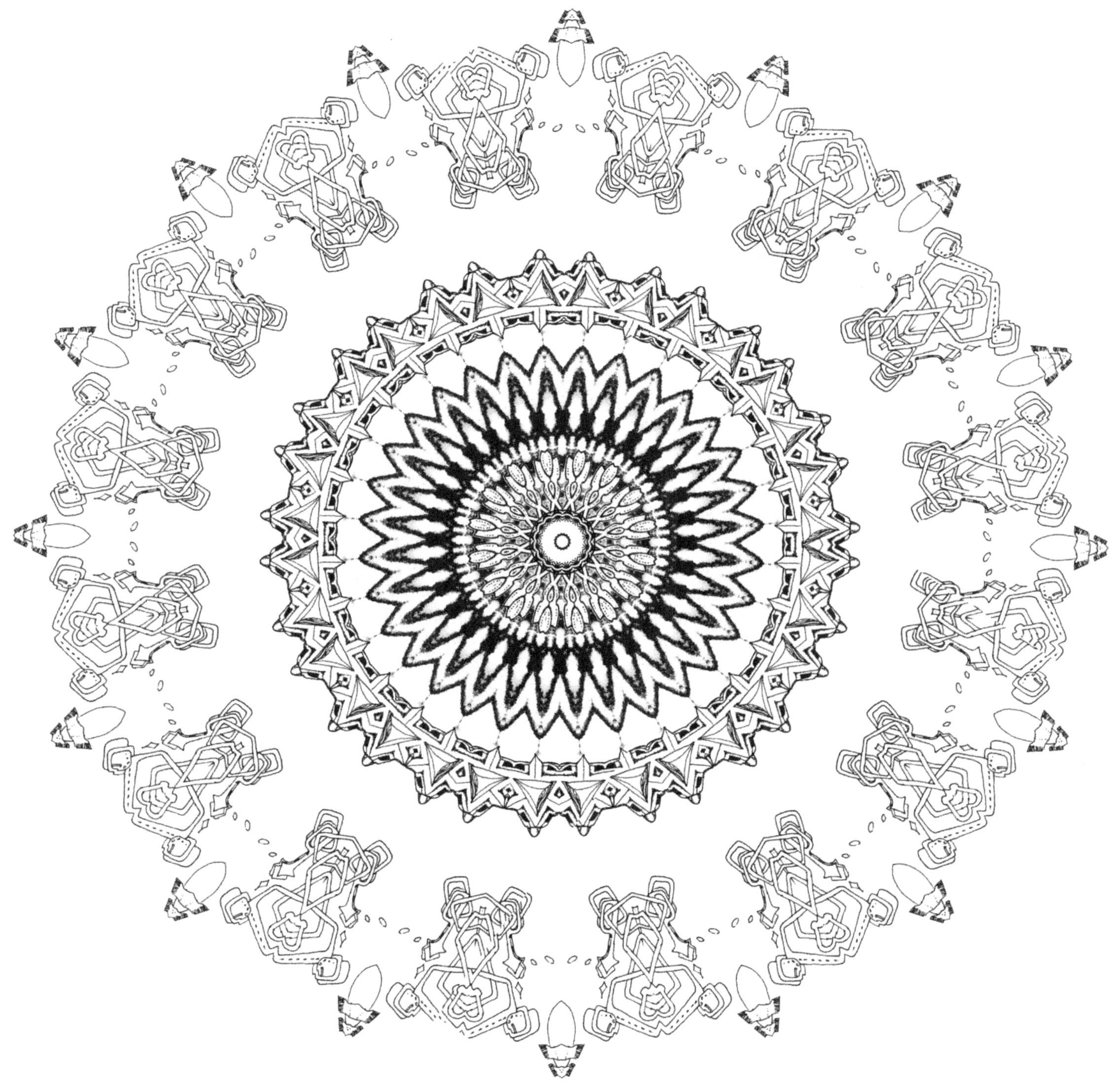

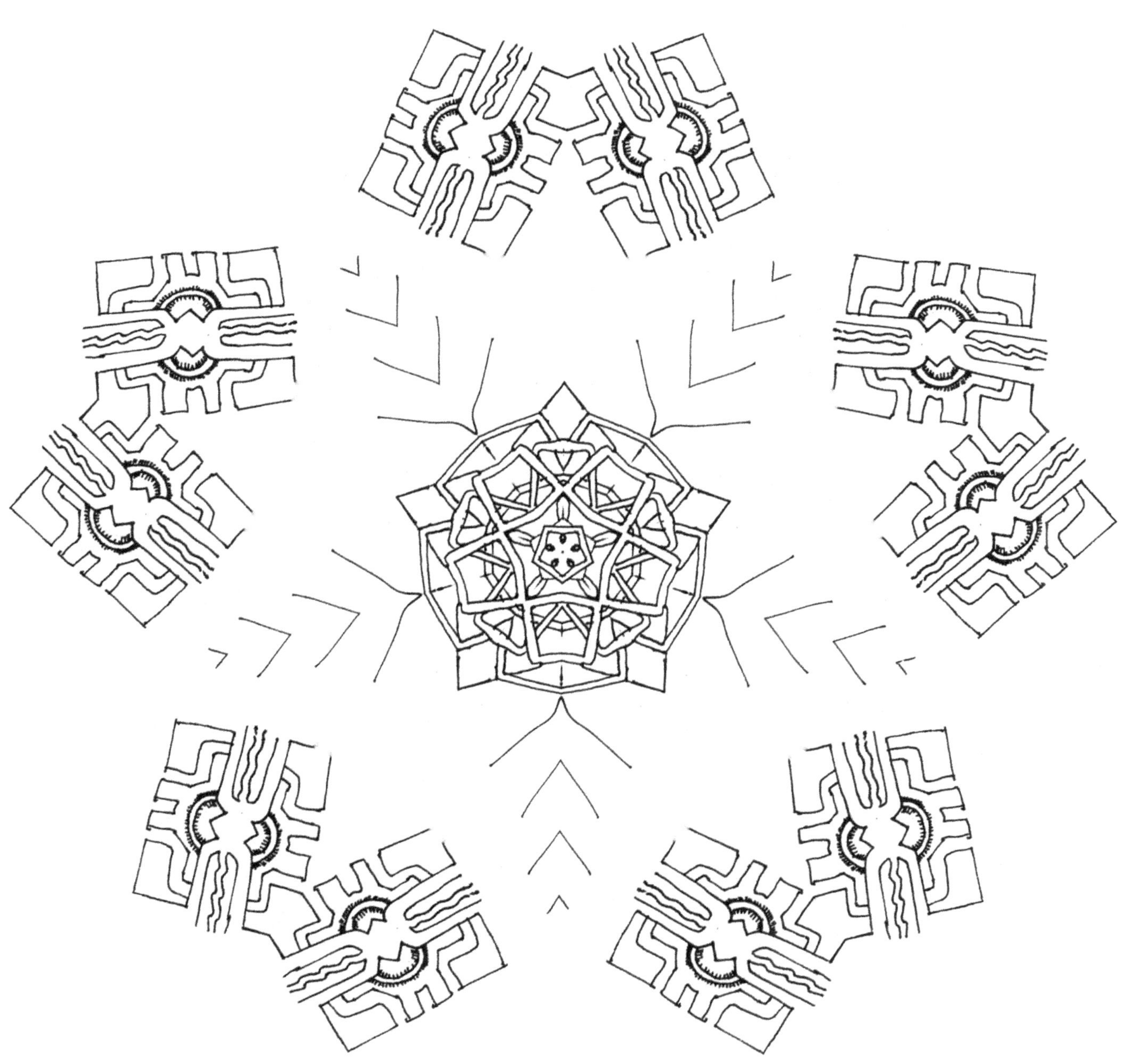

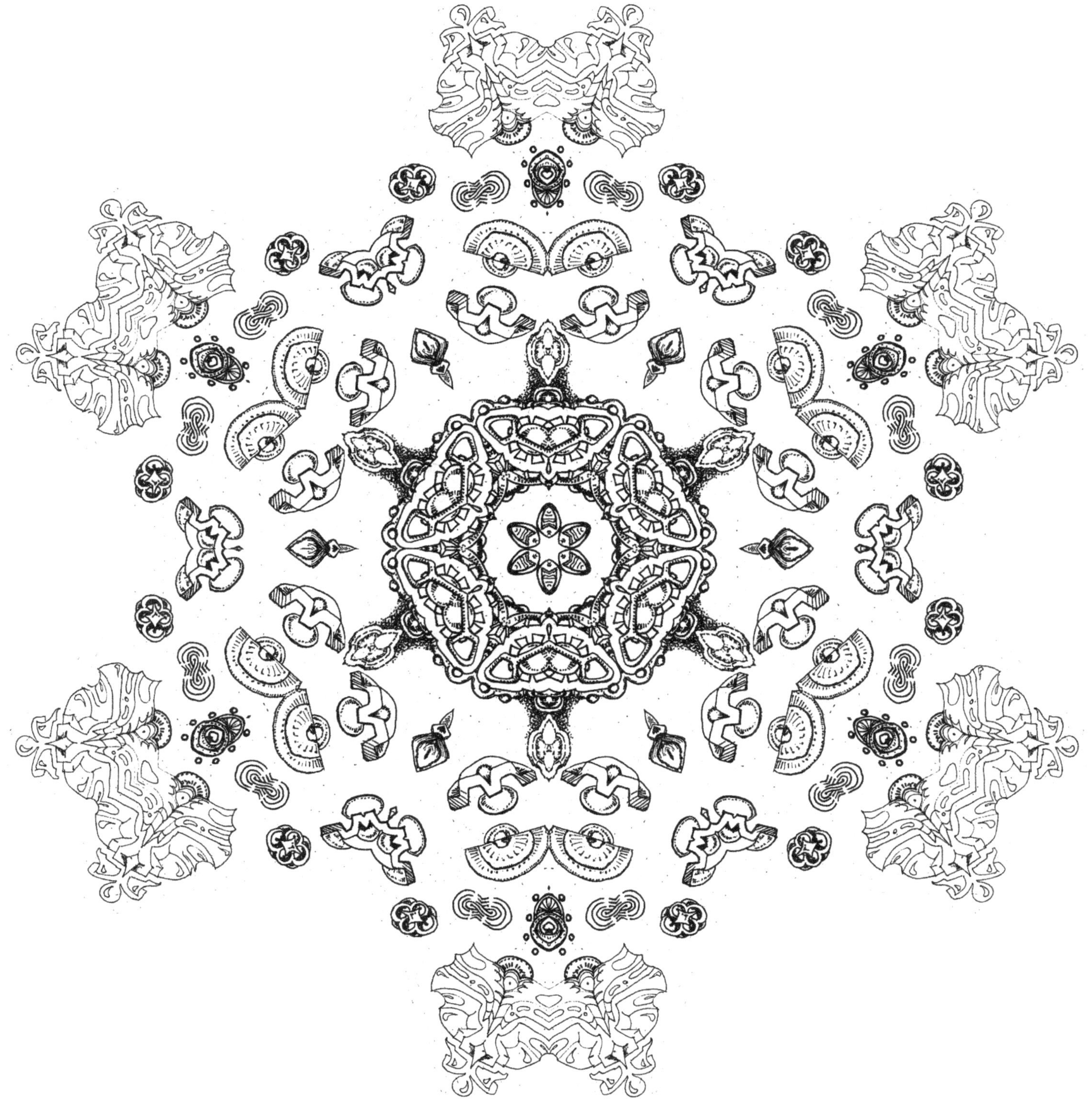

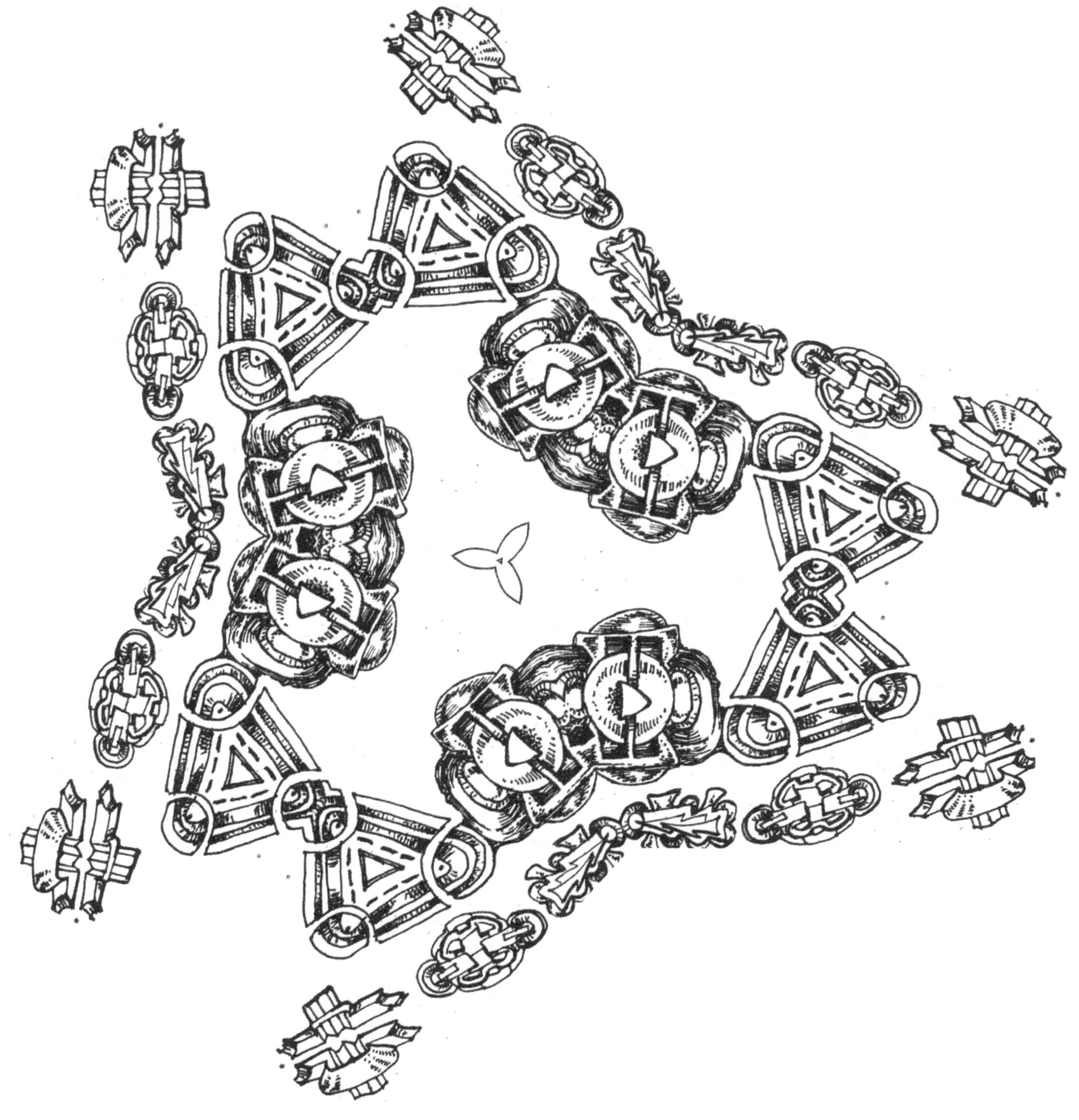

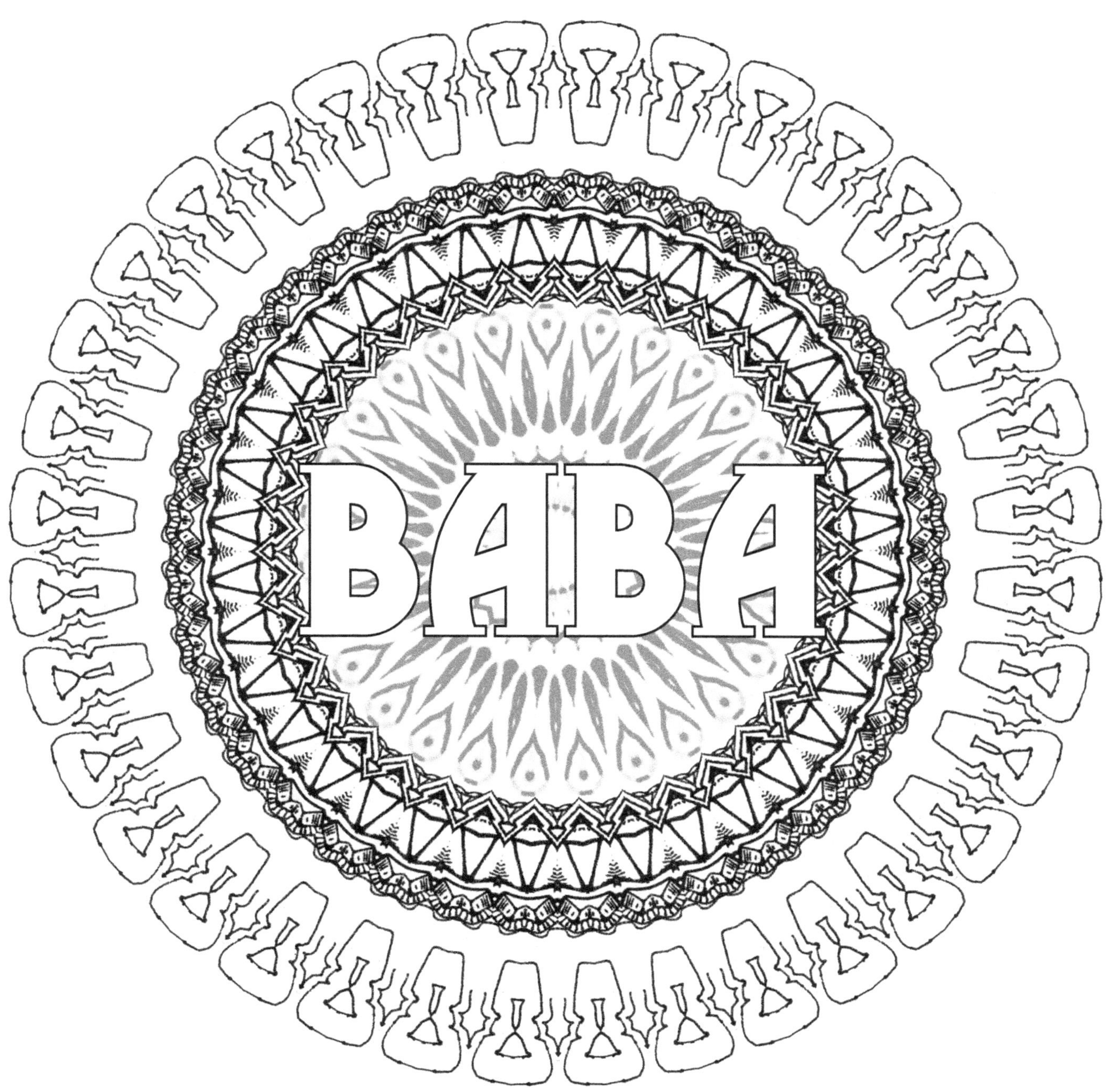
BABA

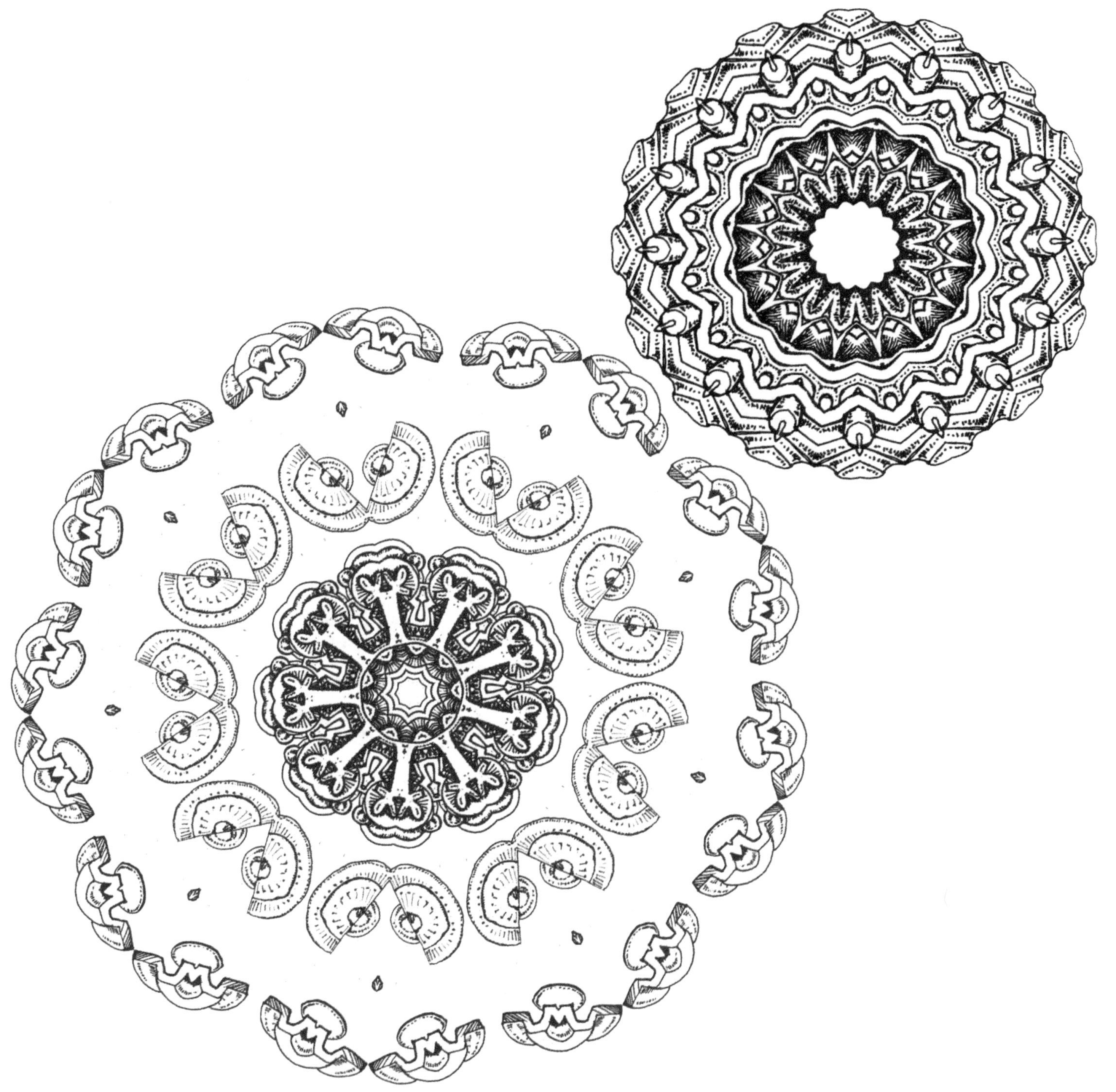

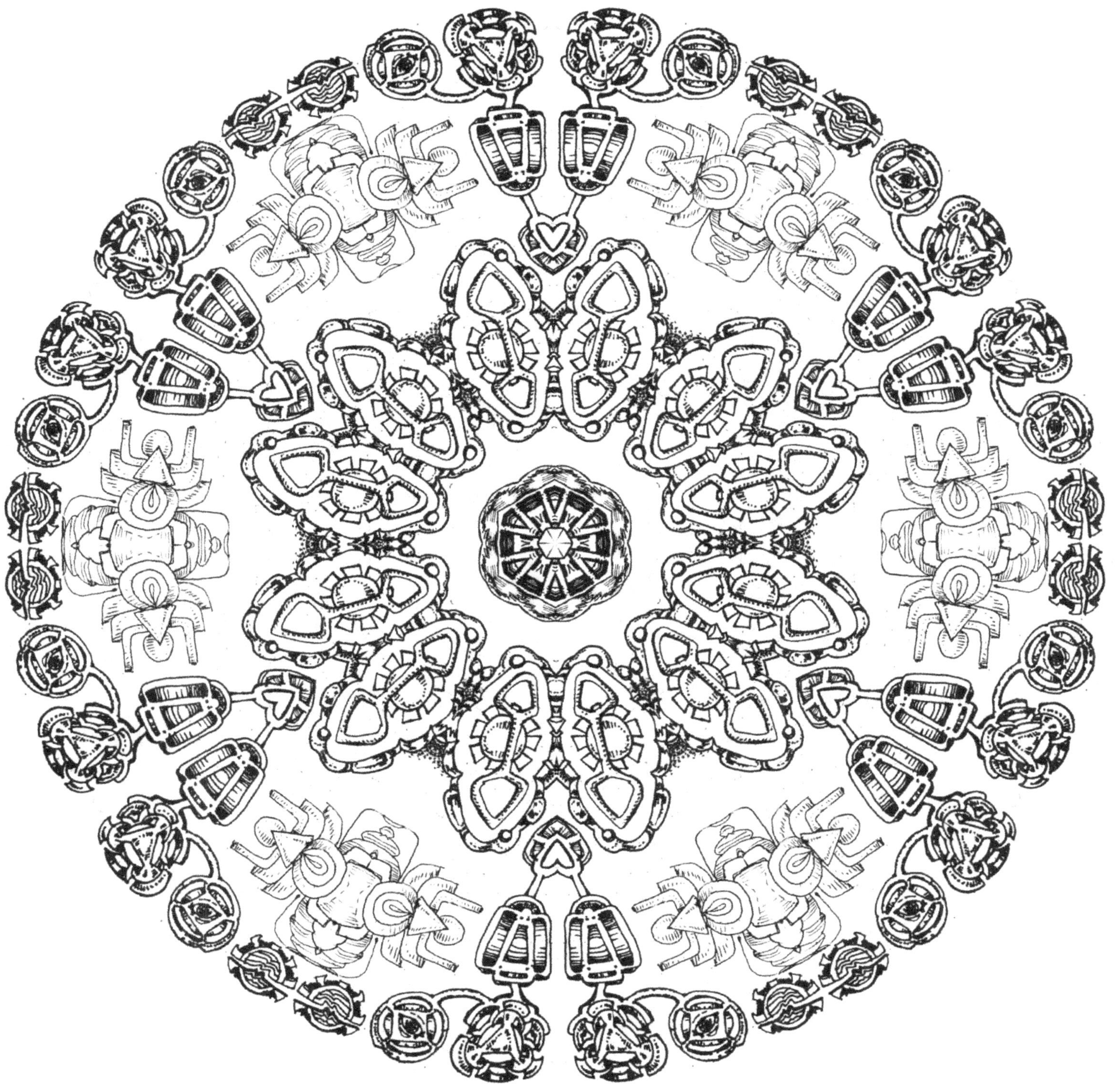

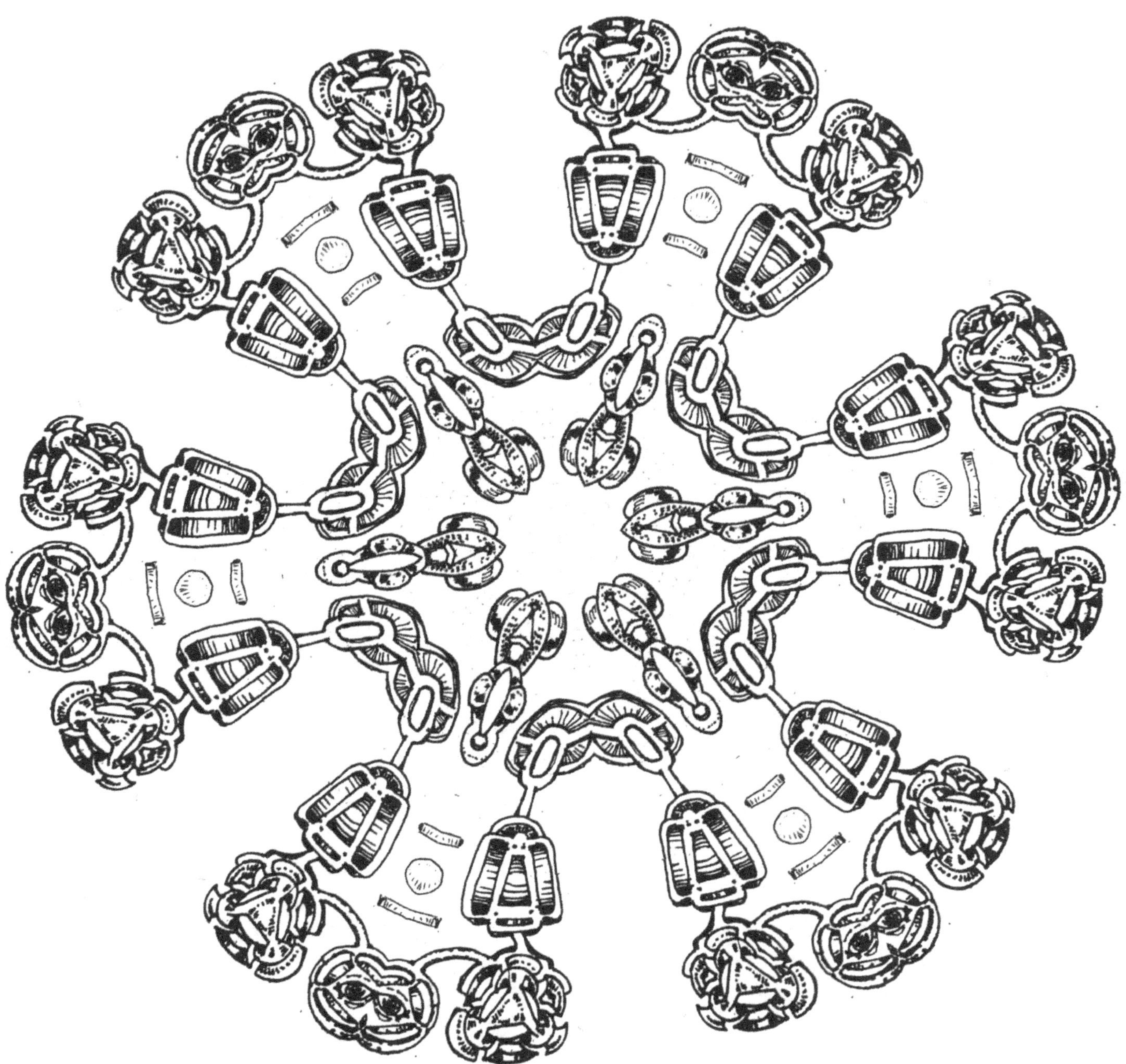

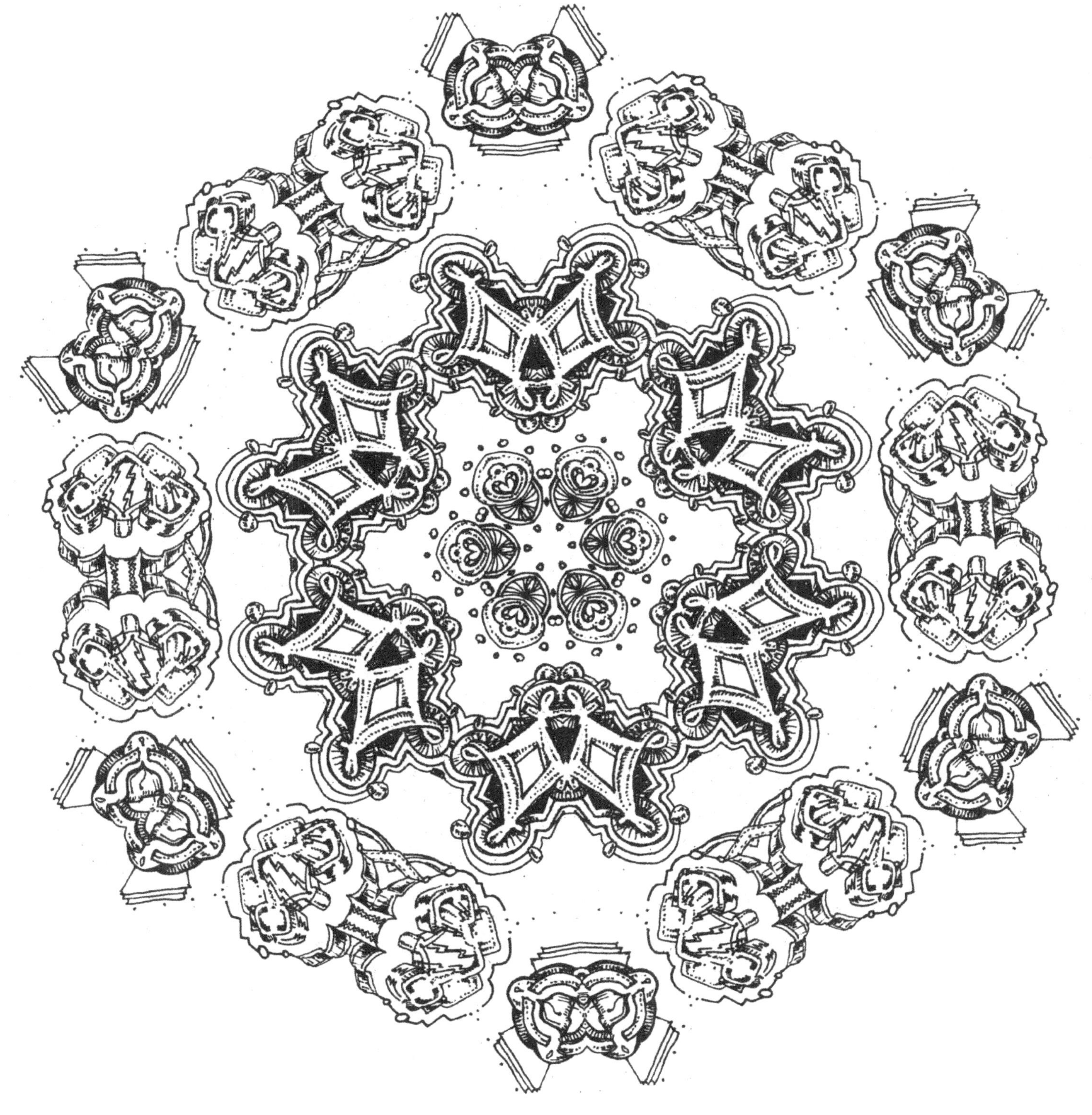

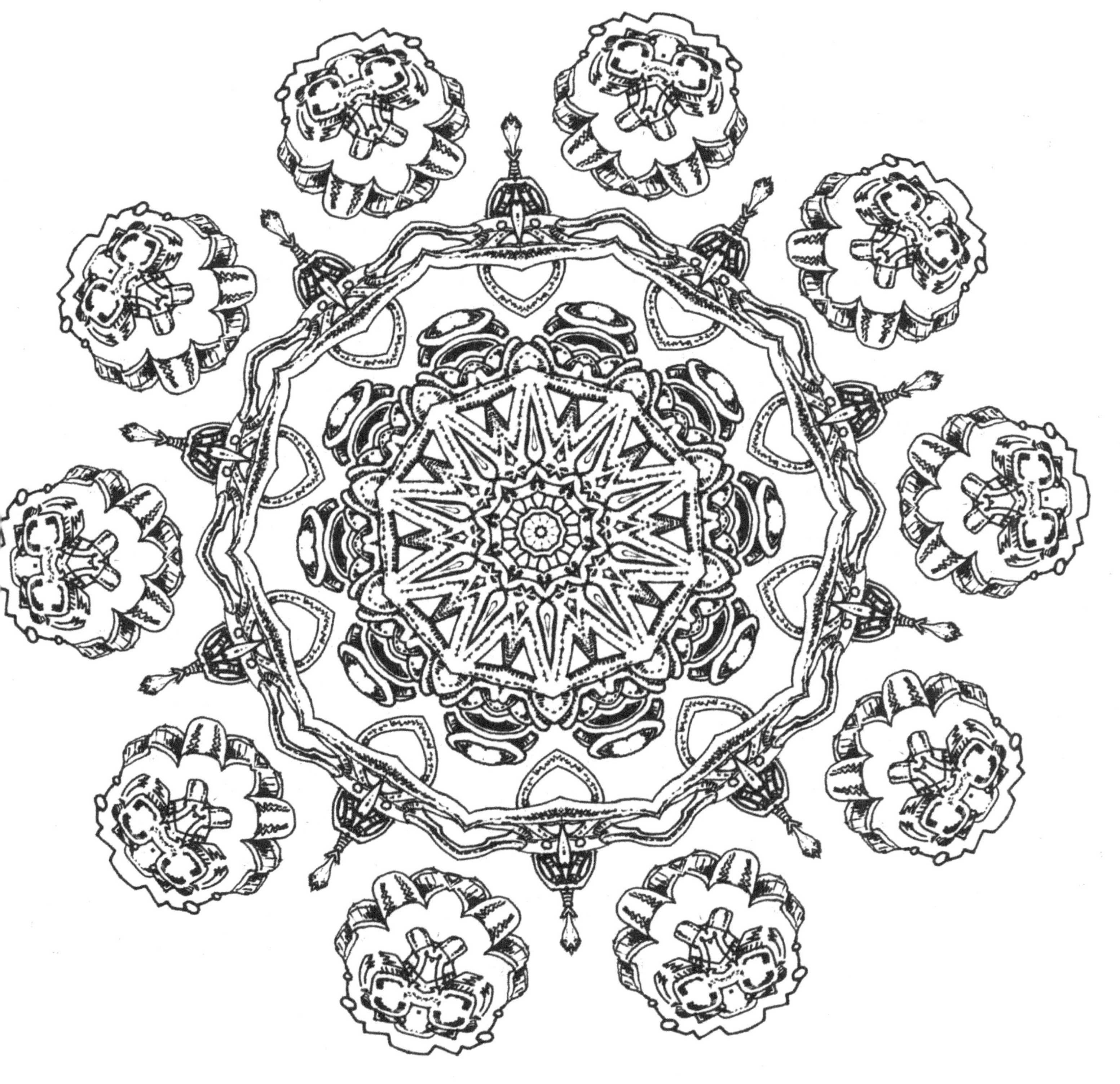

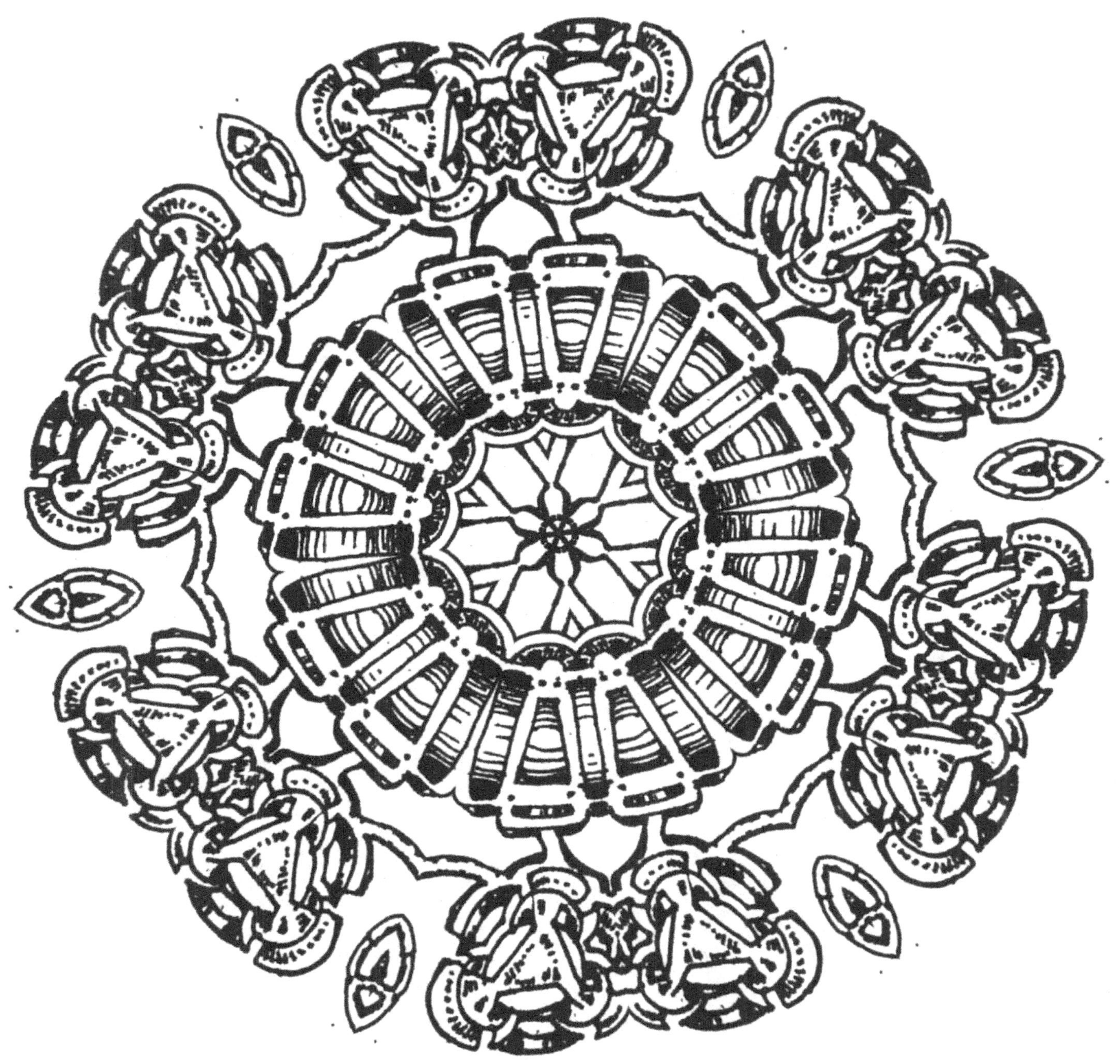

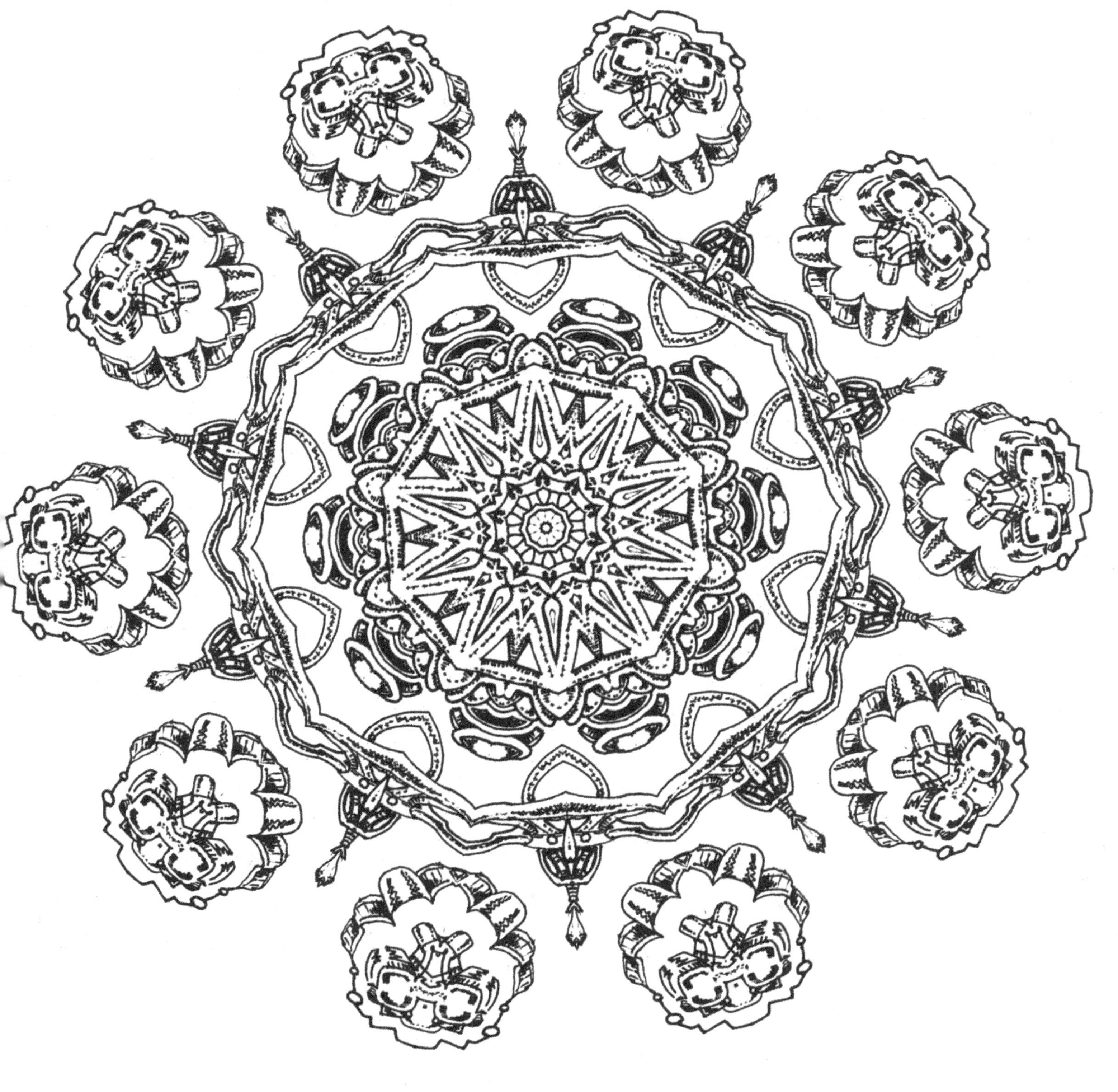

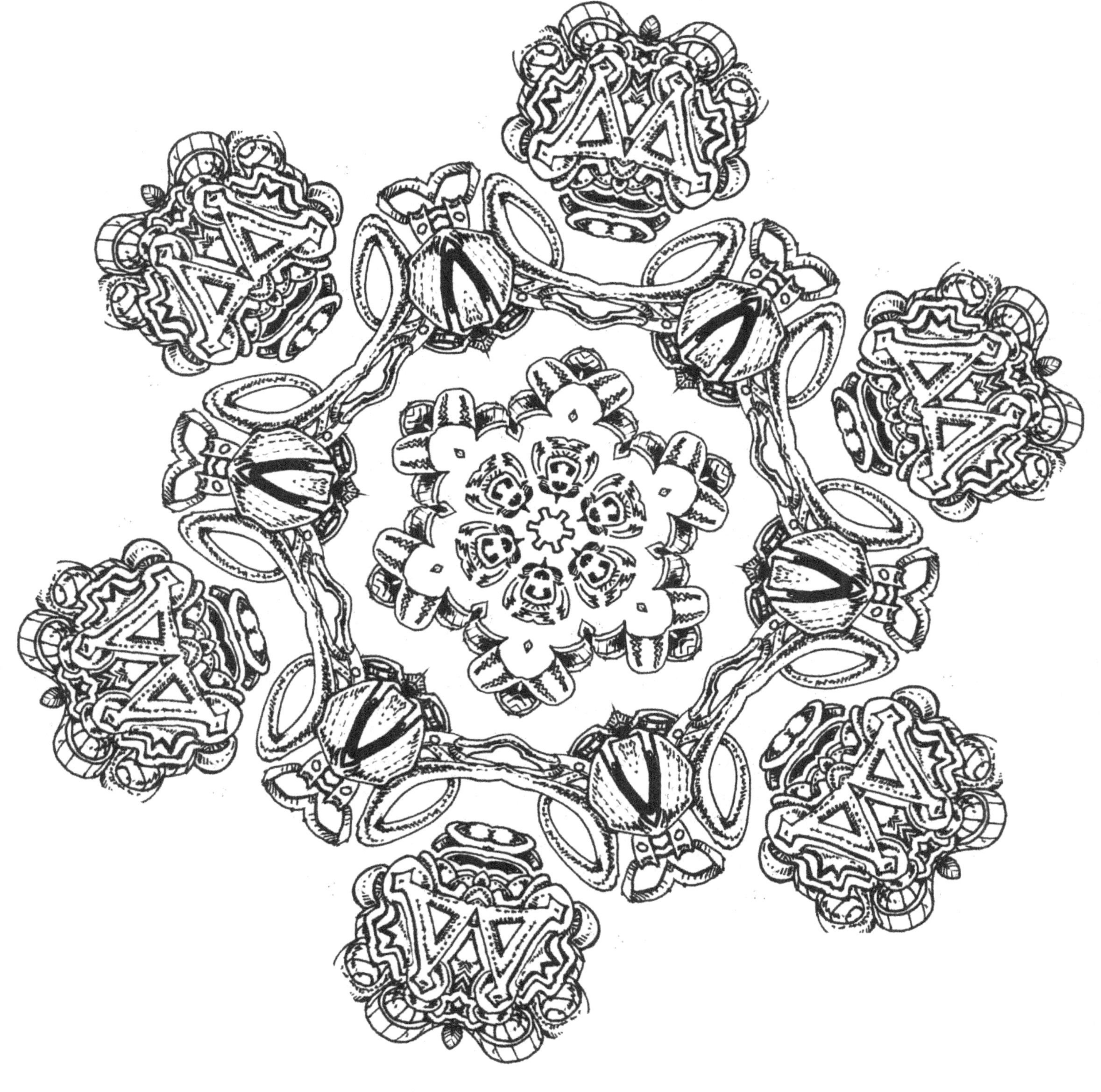

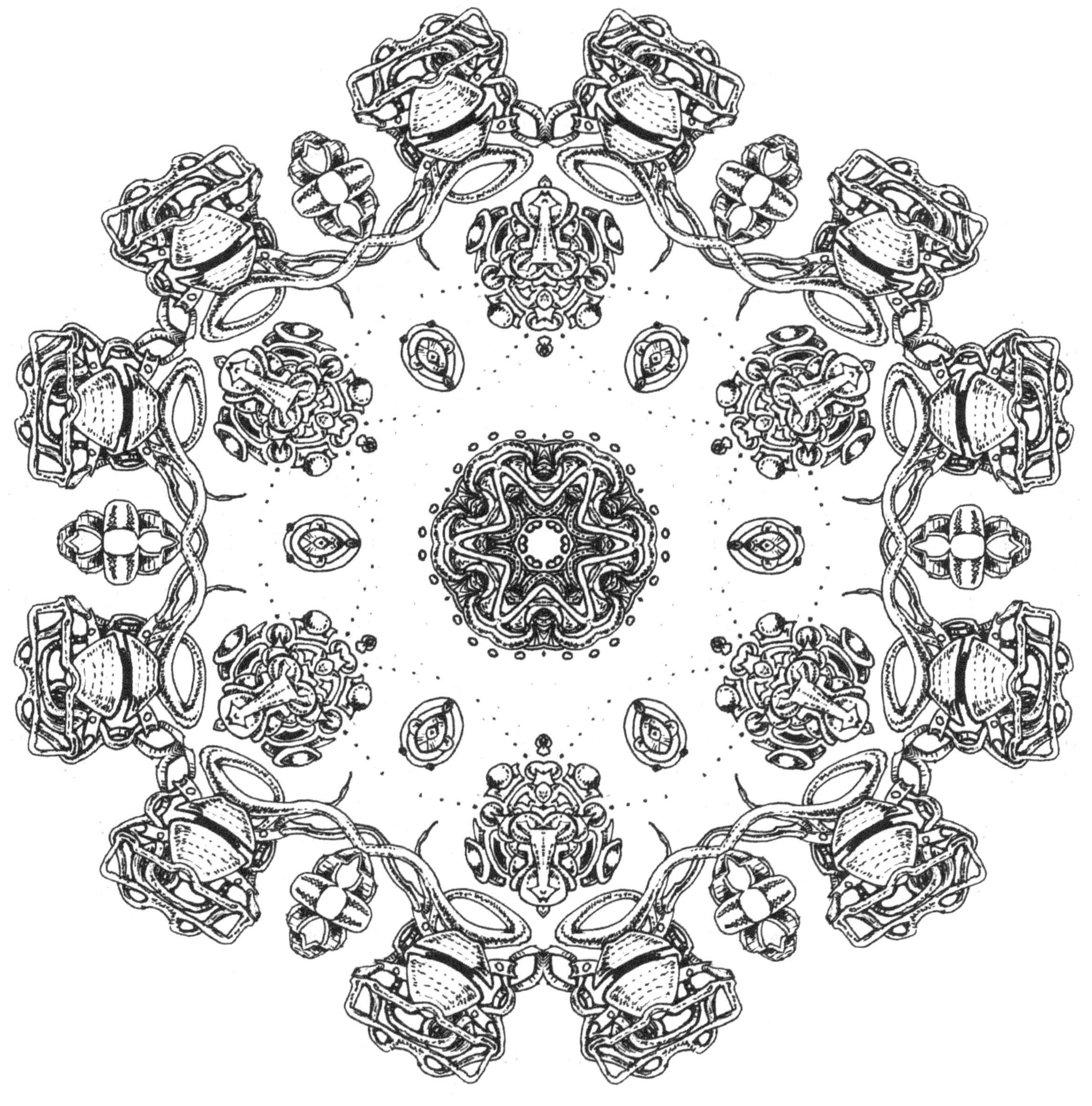

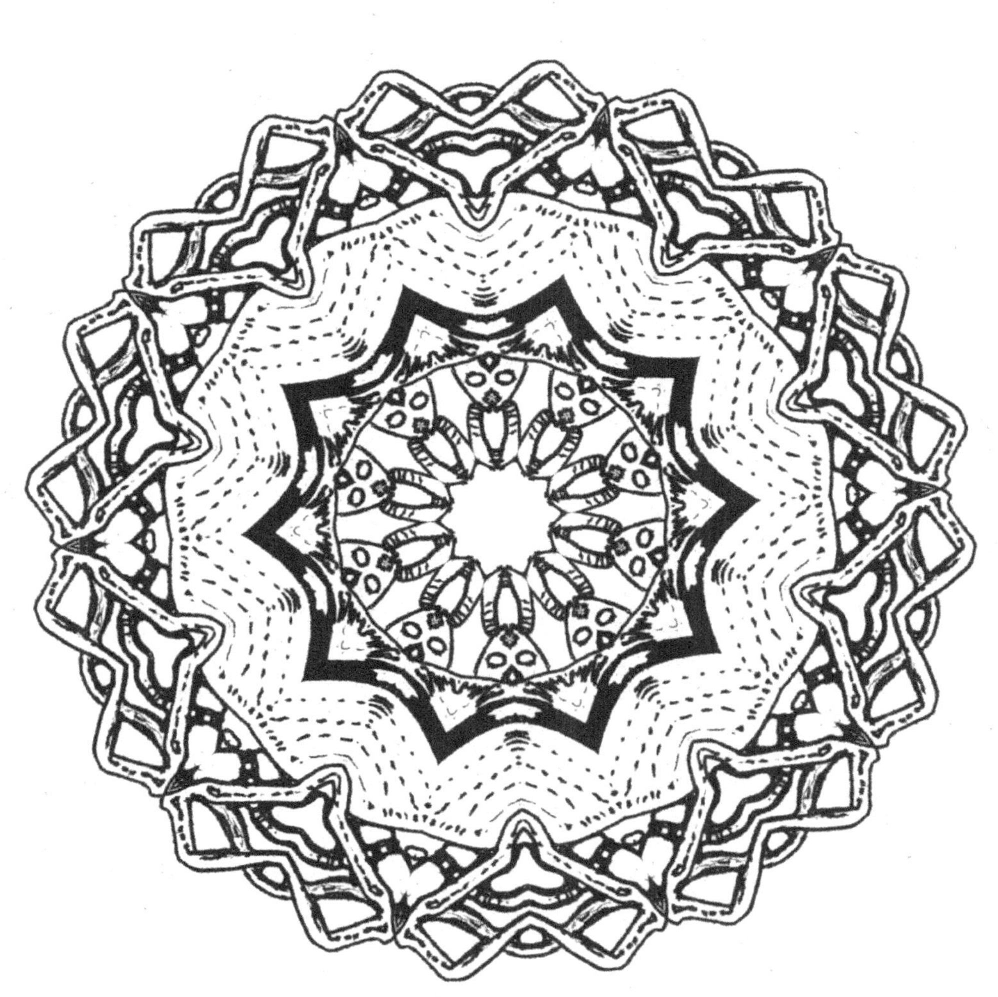

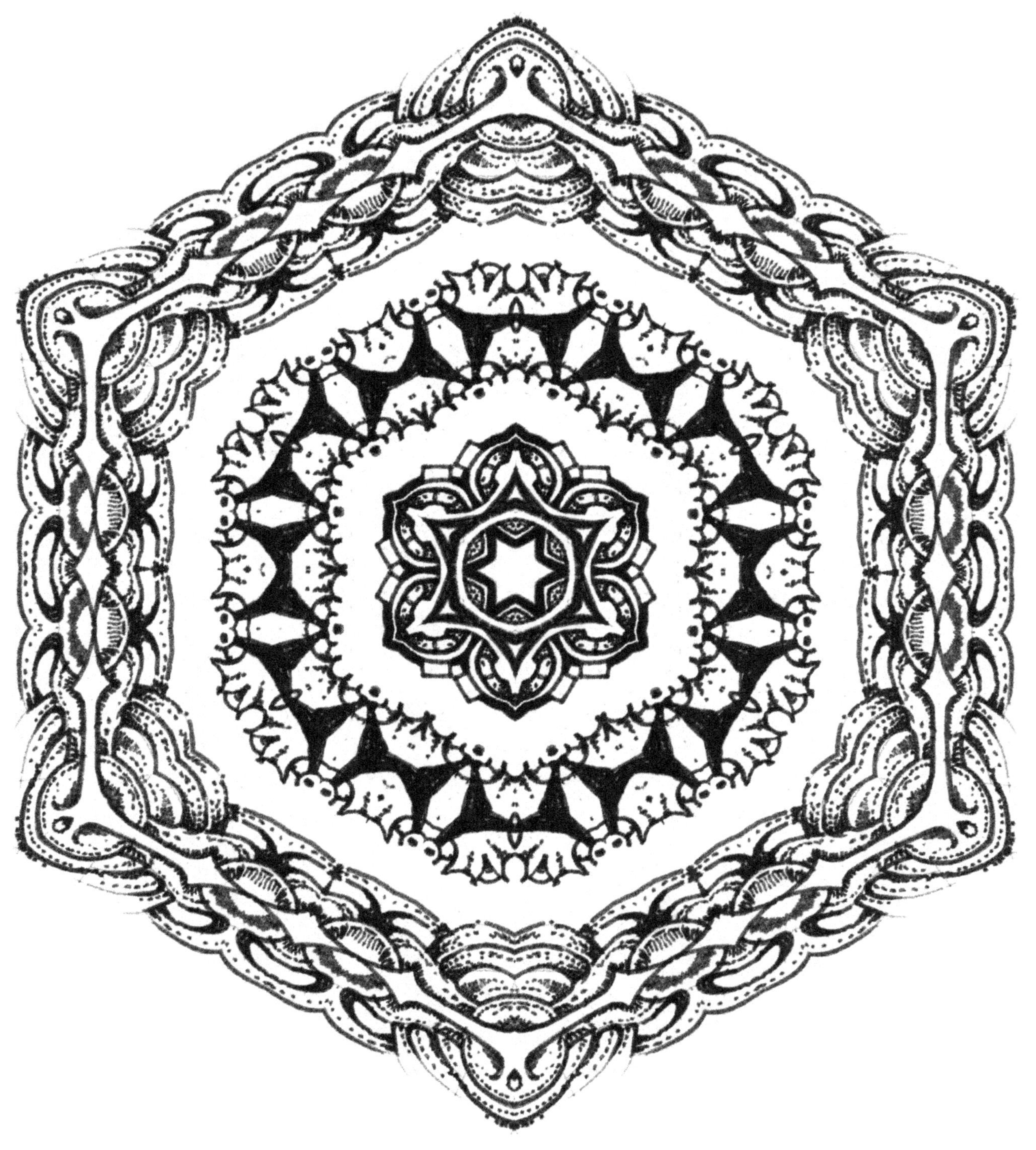

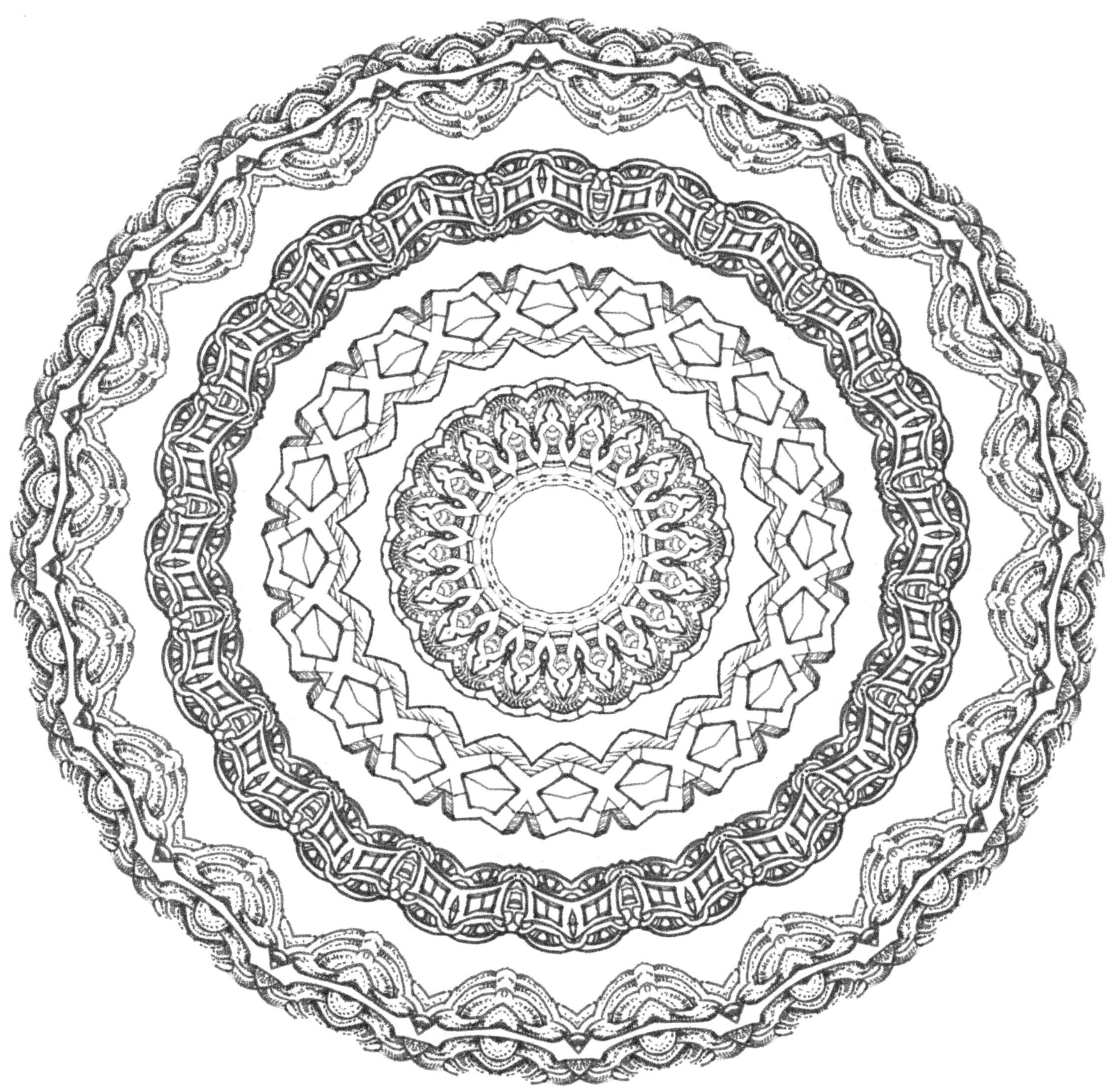

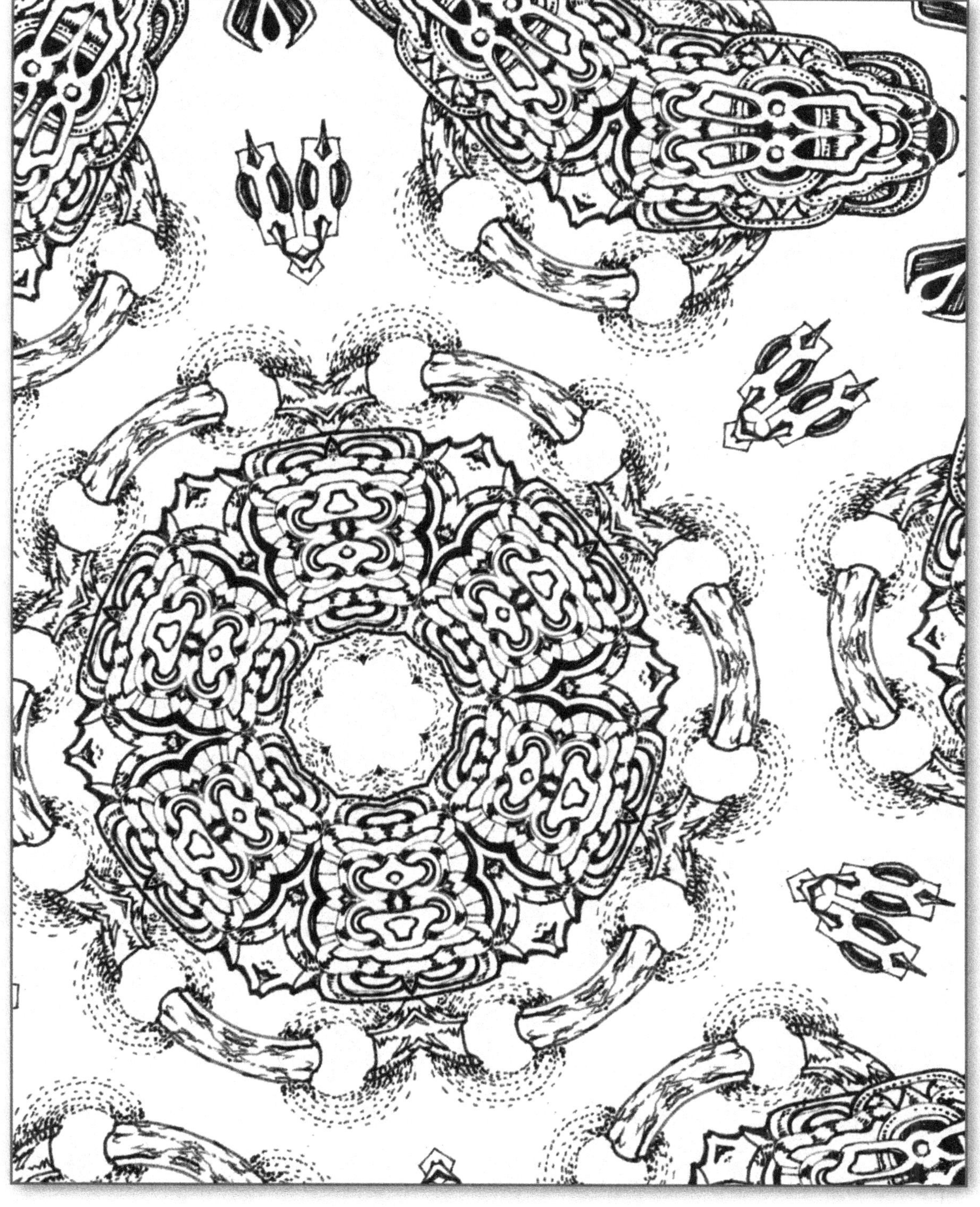

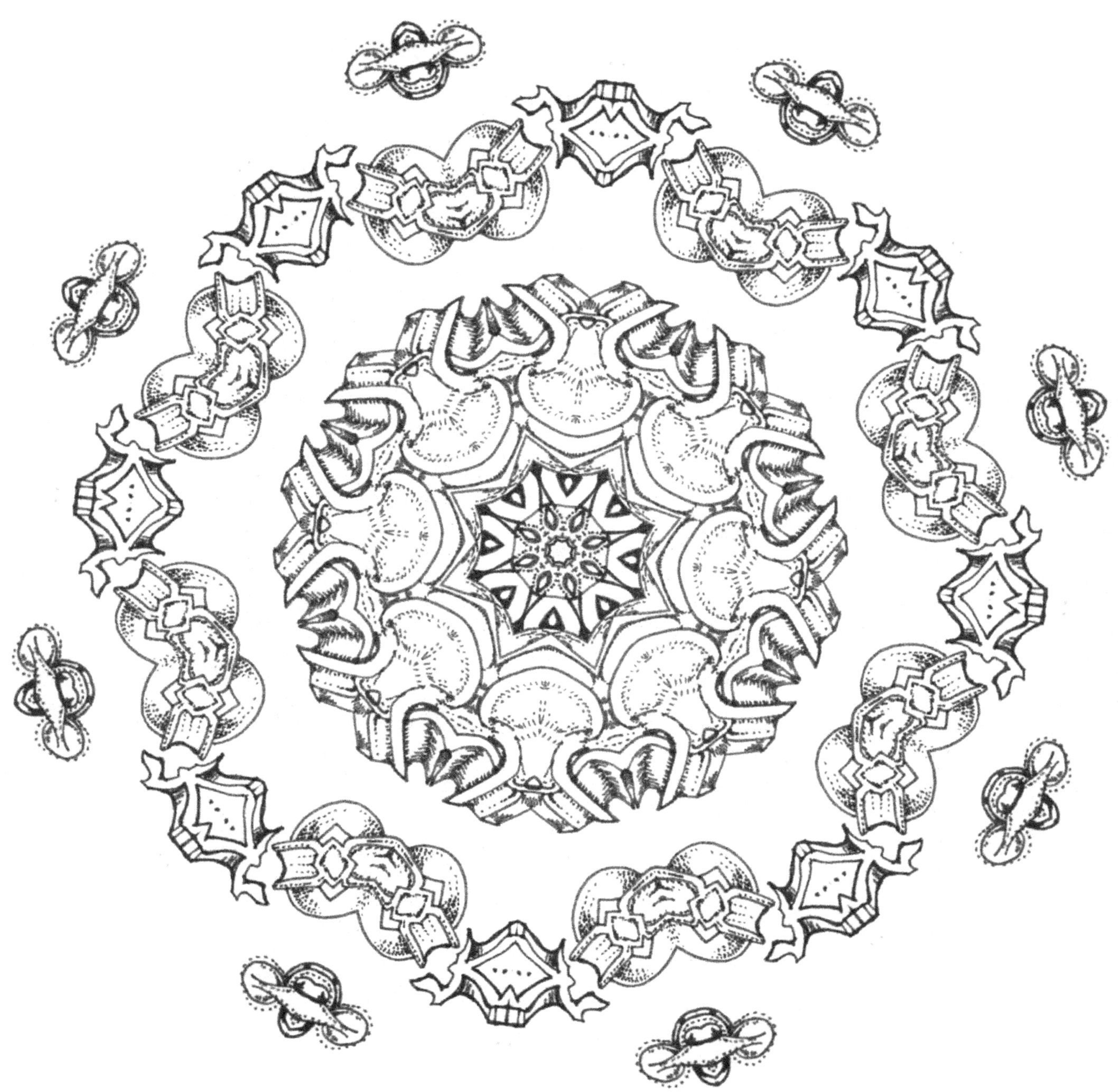

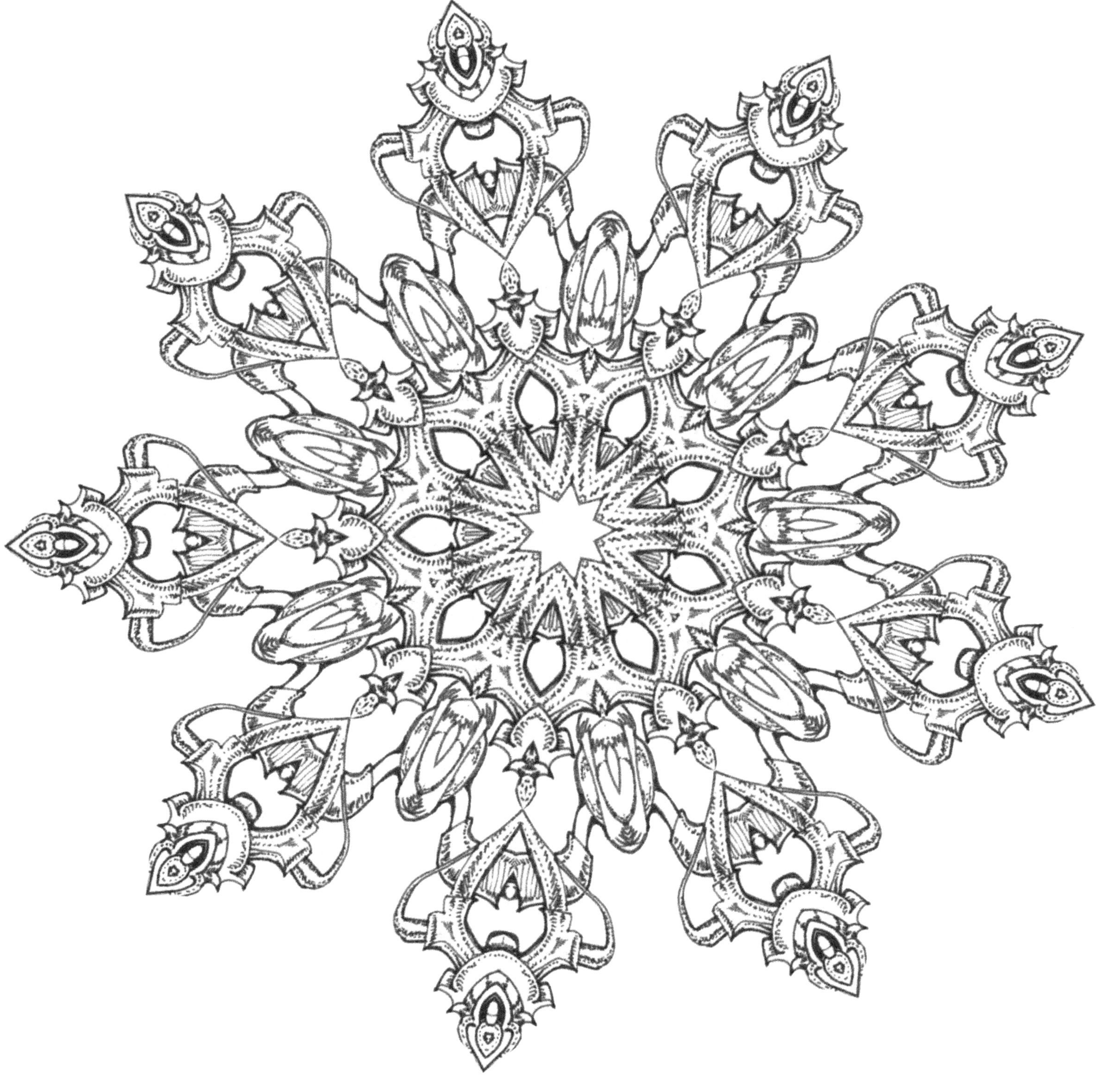

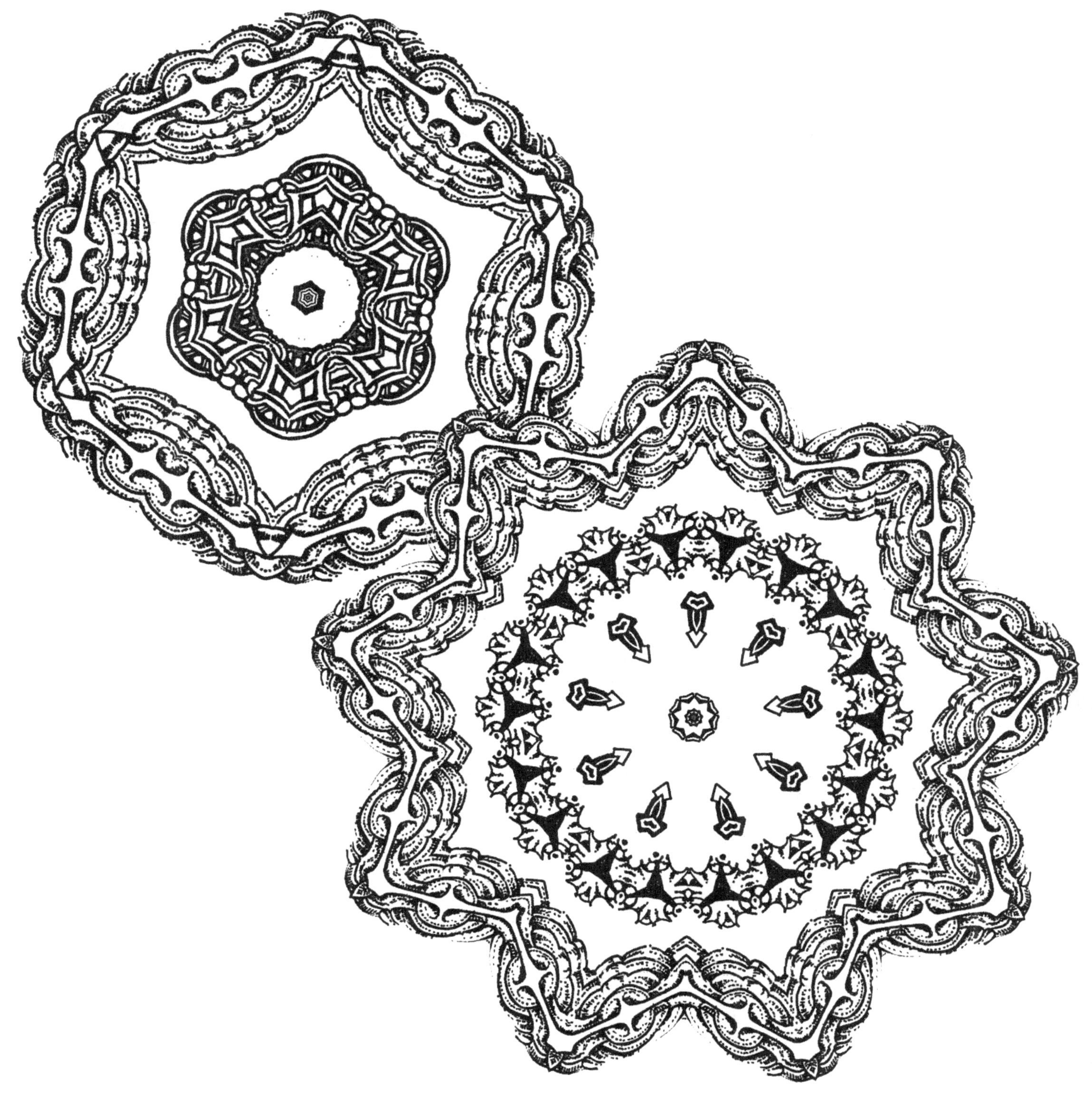

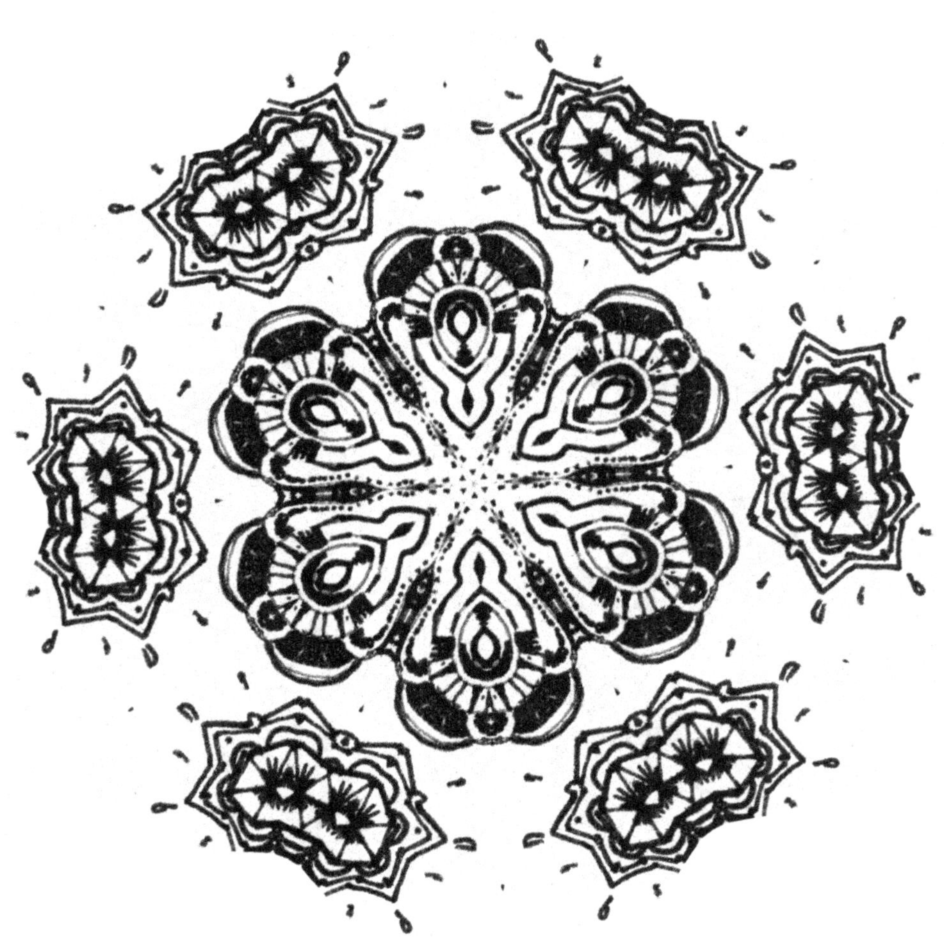

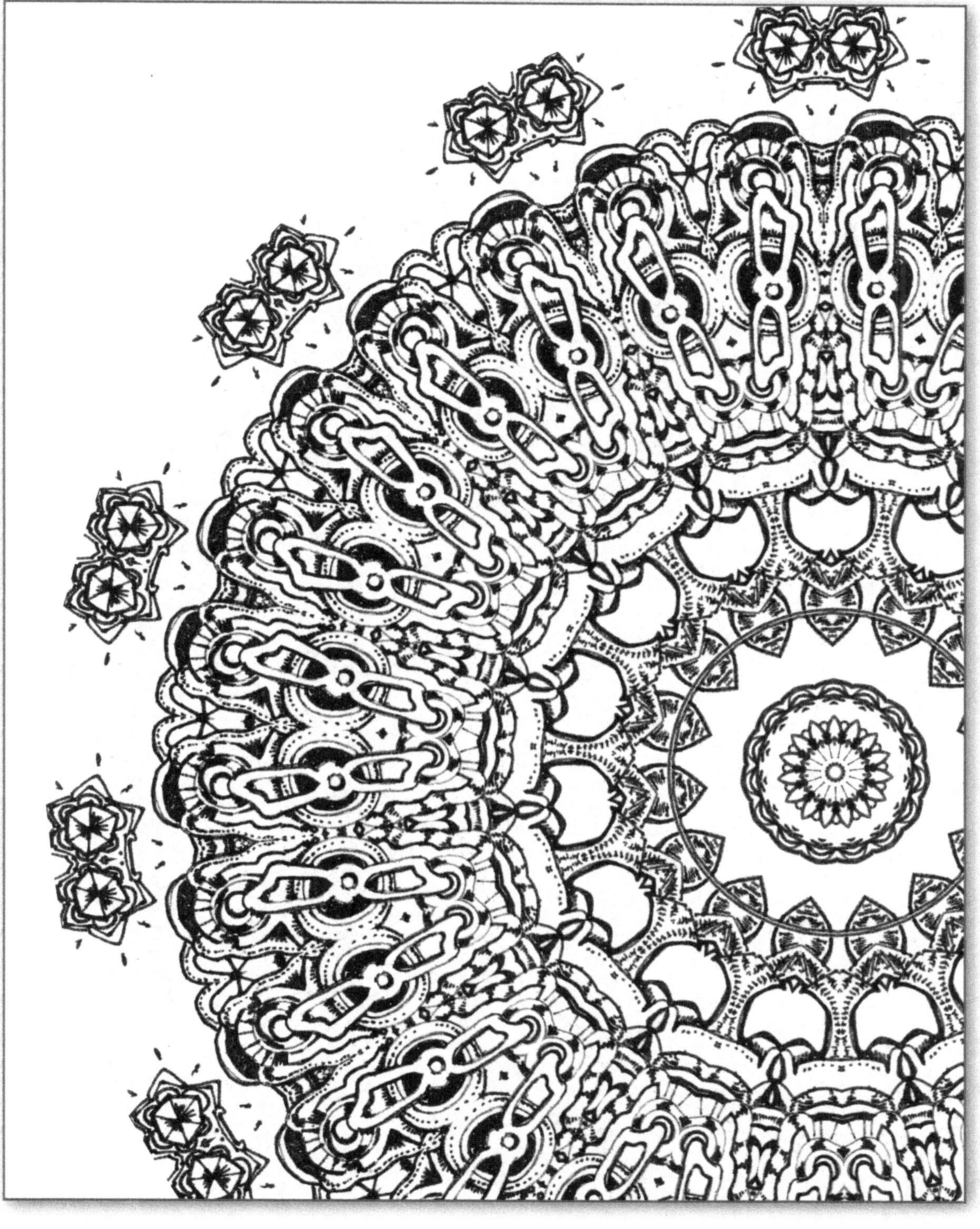

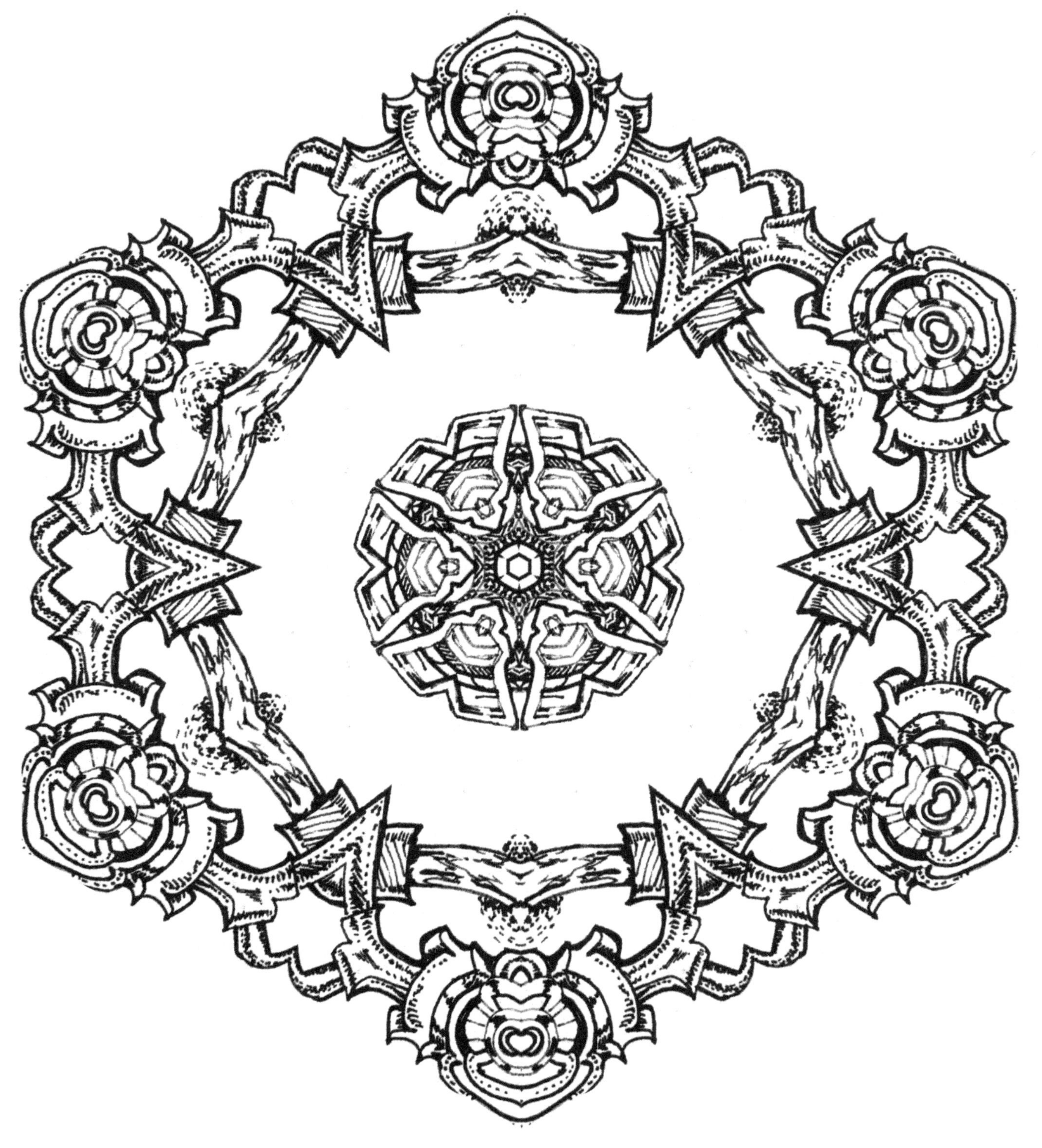

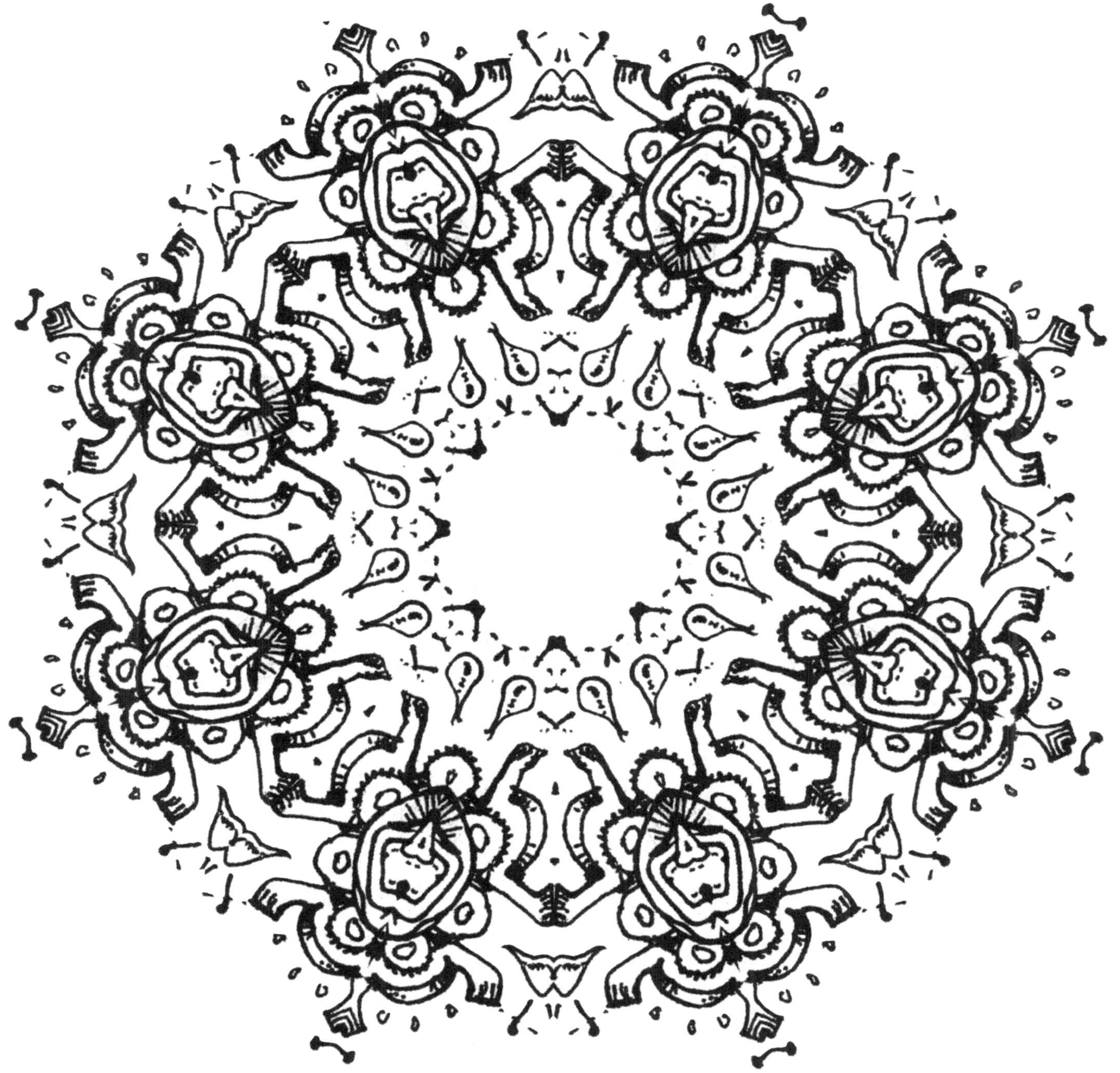

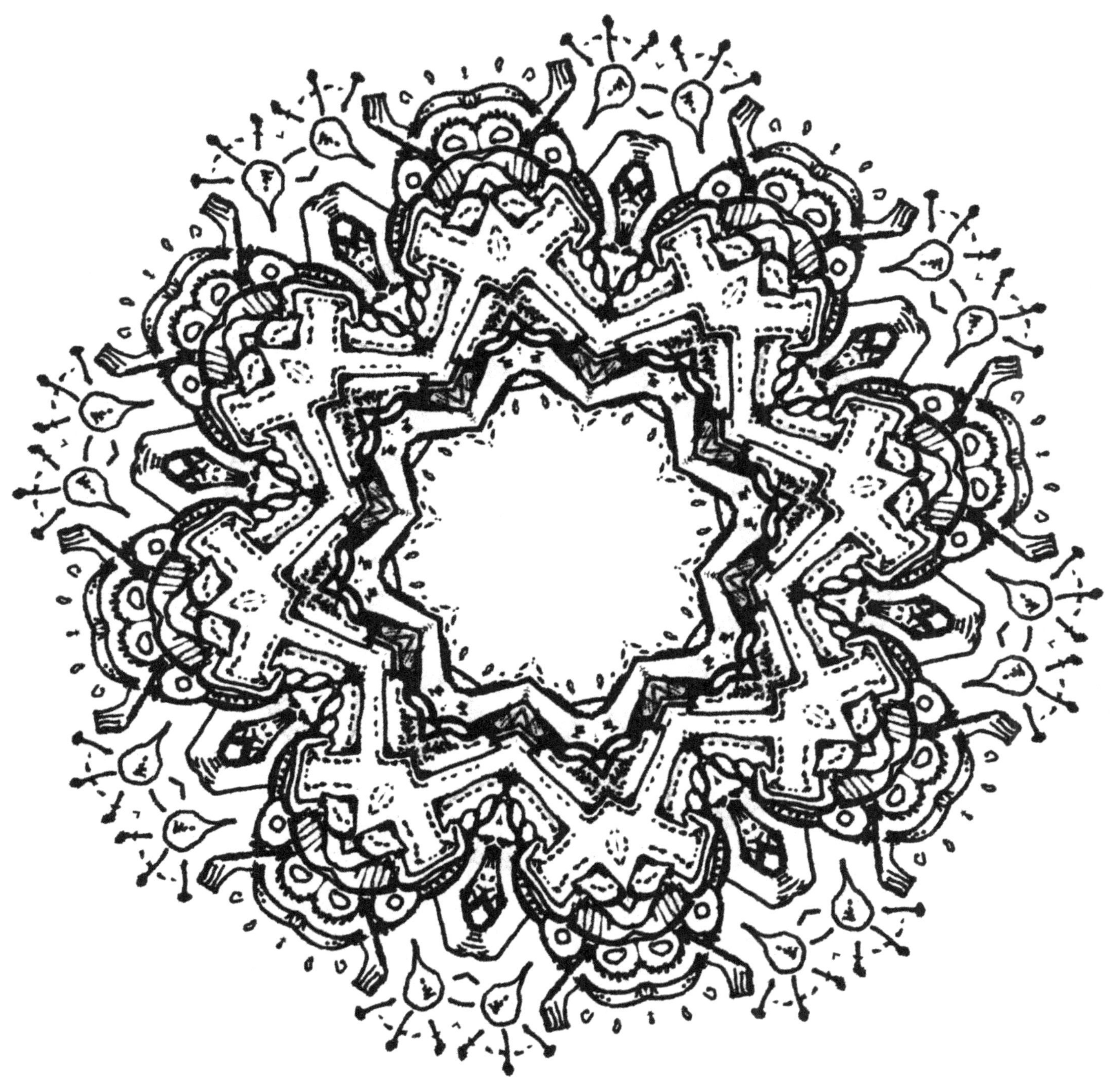

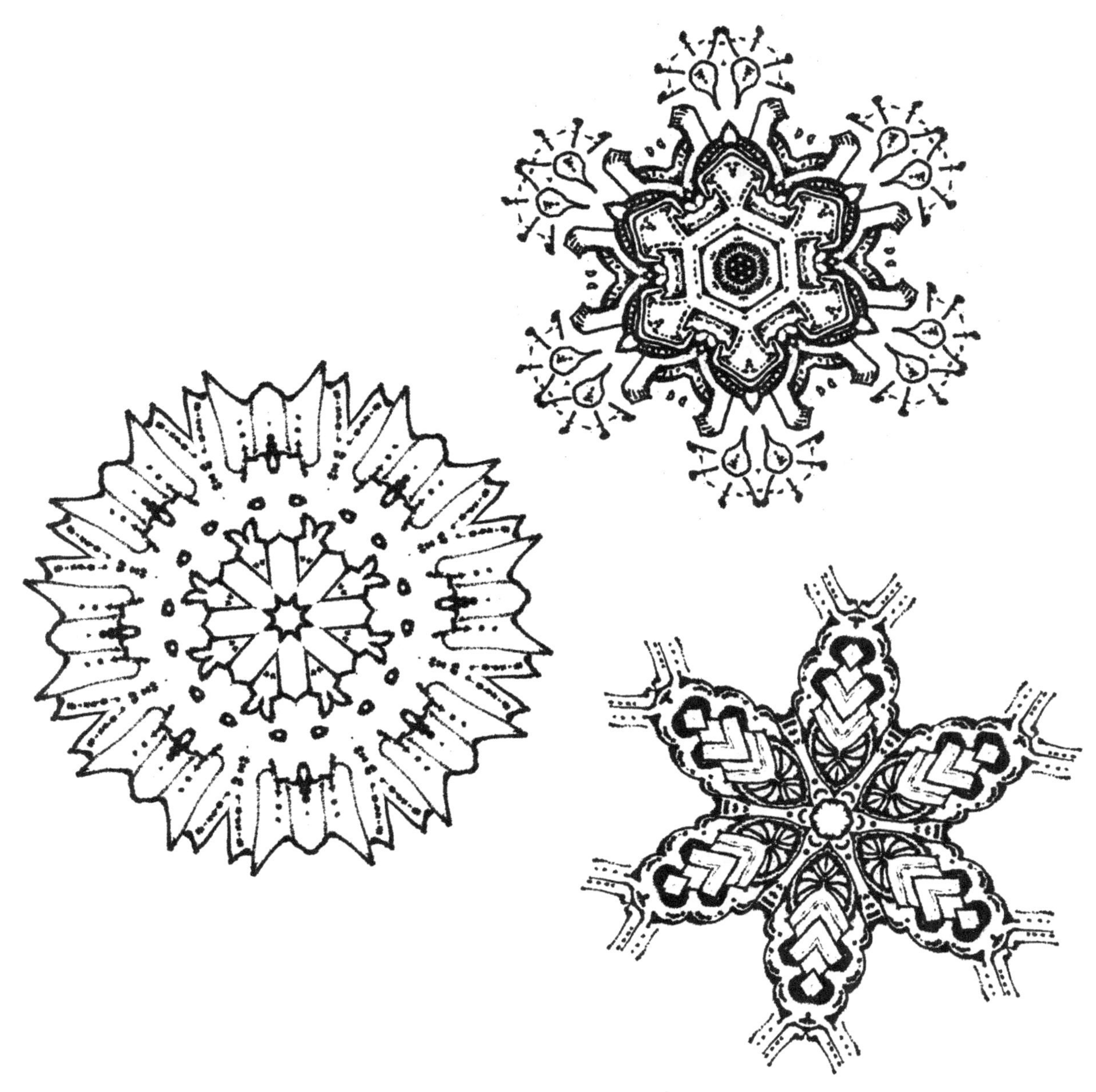

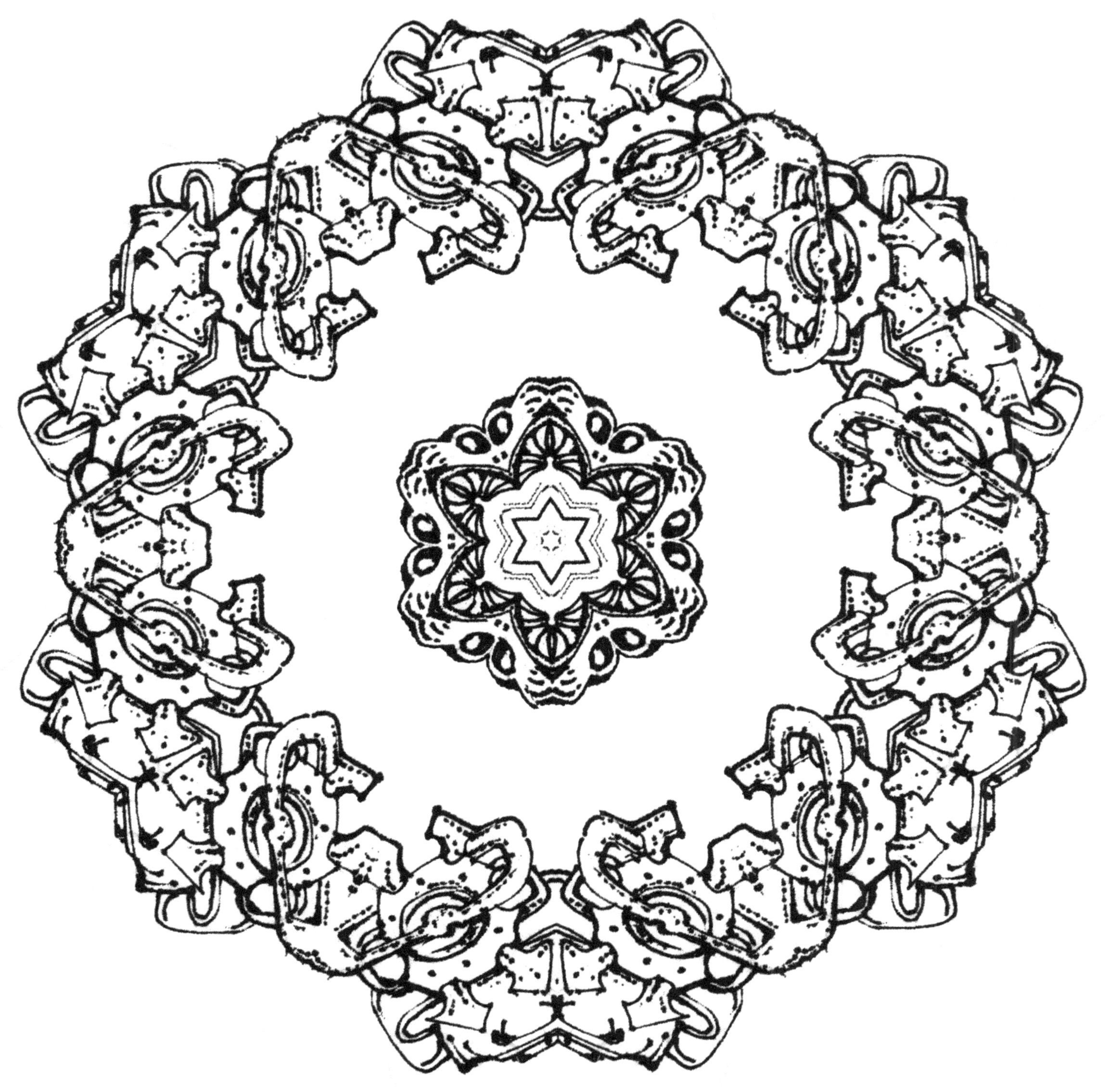

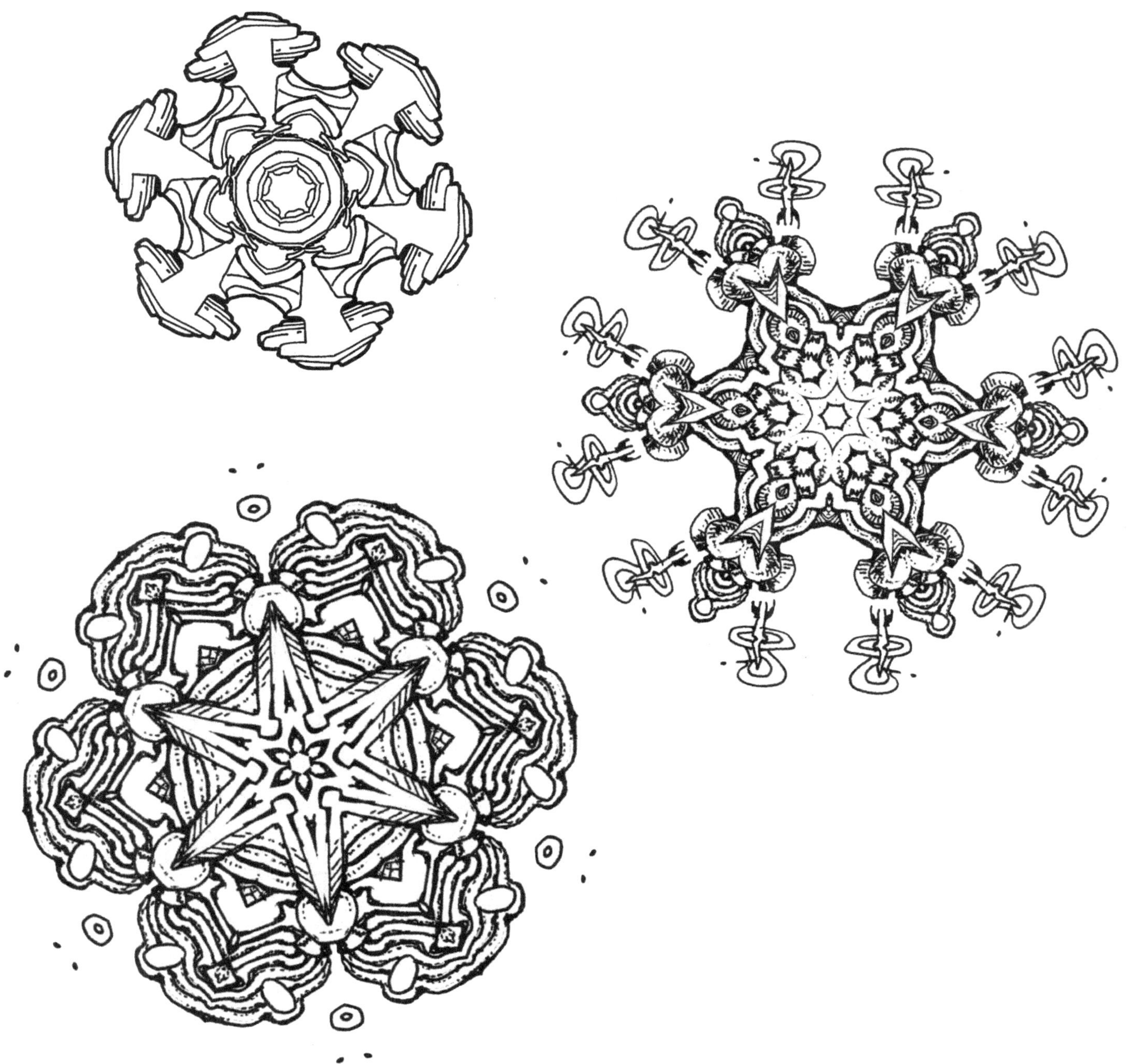

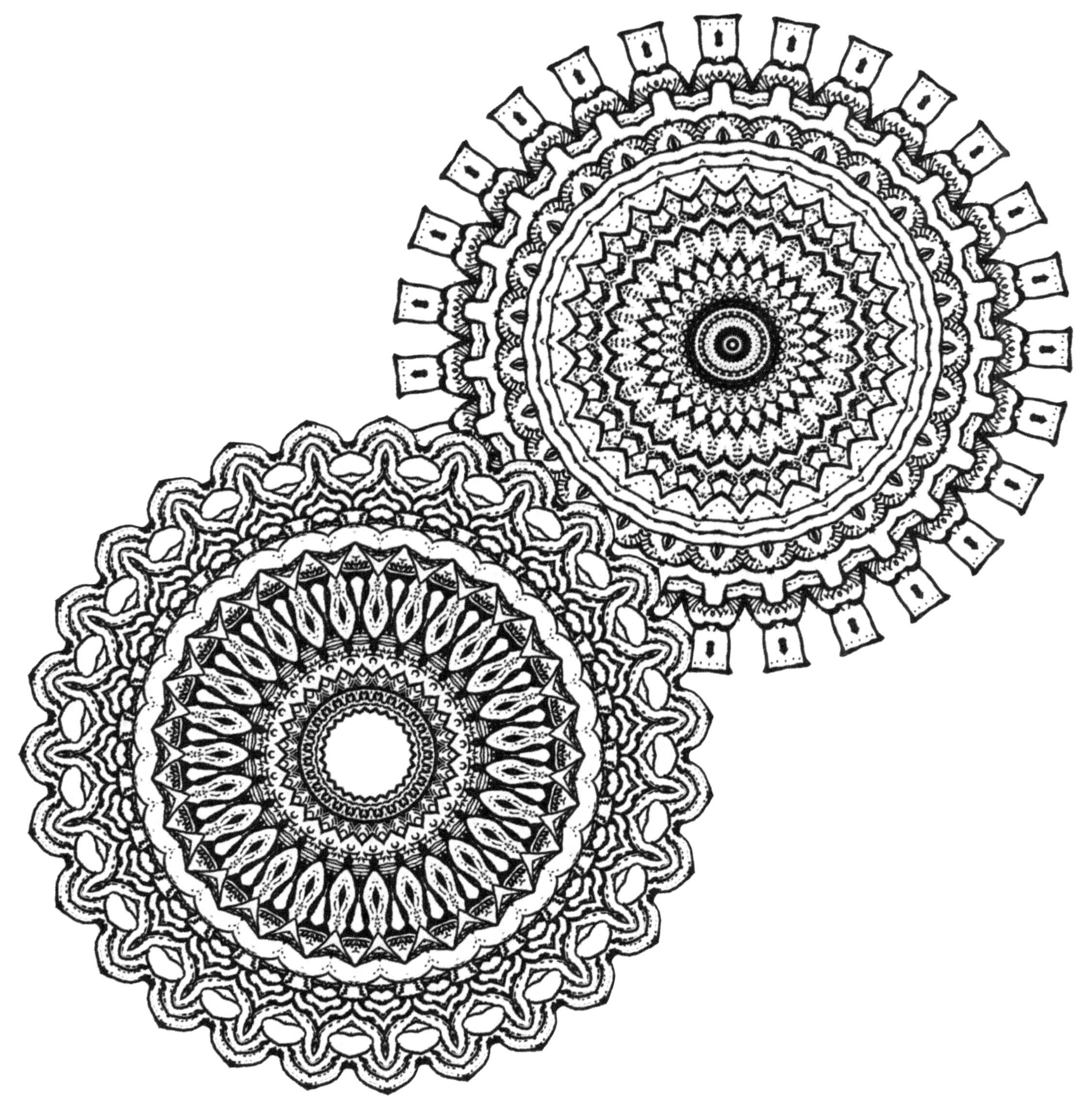

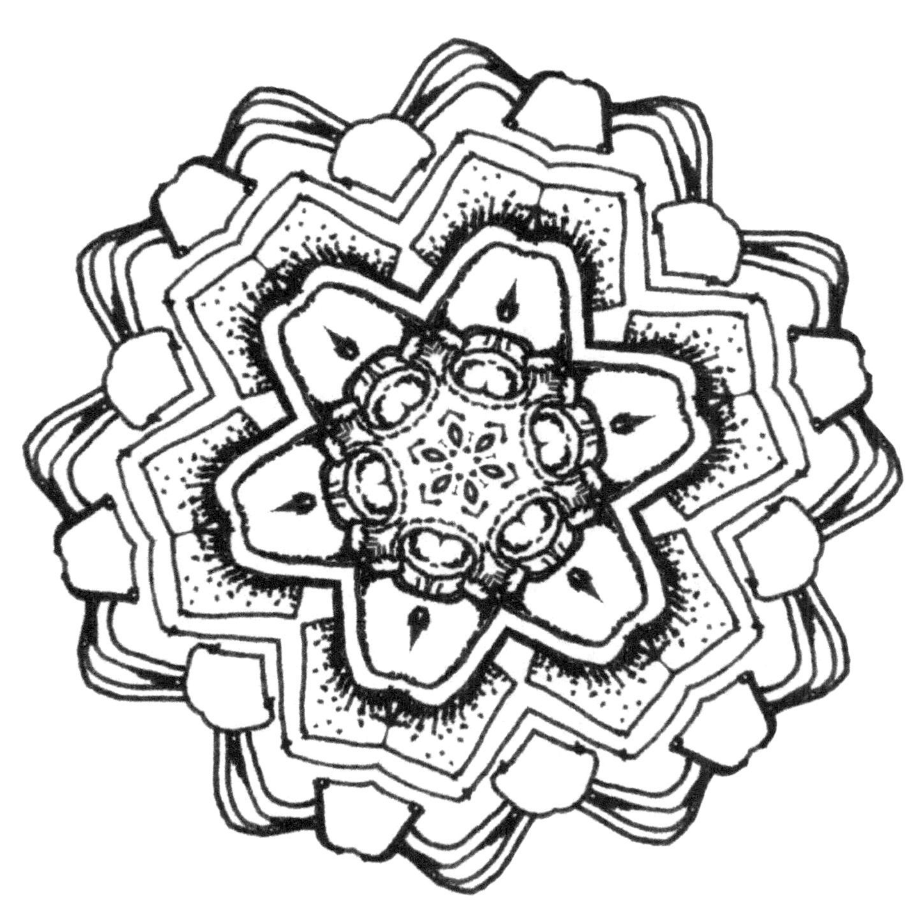

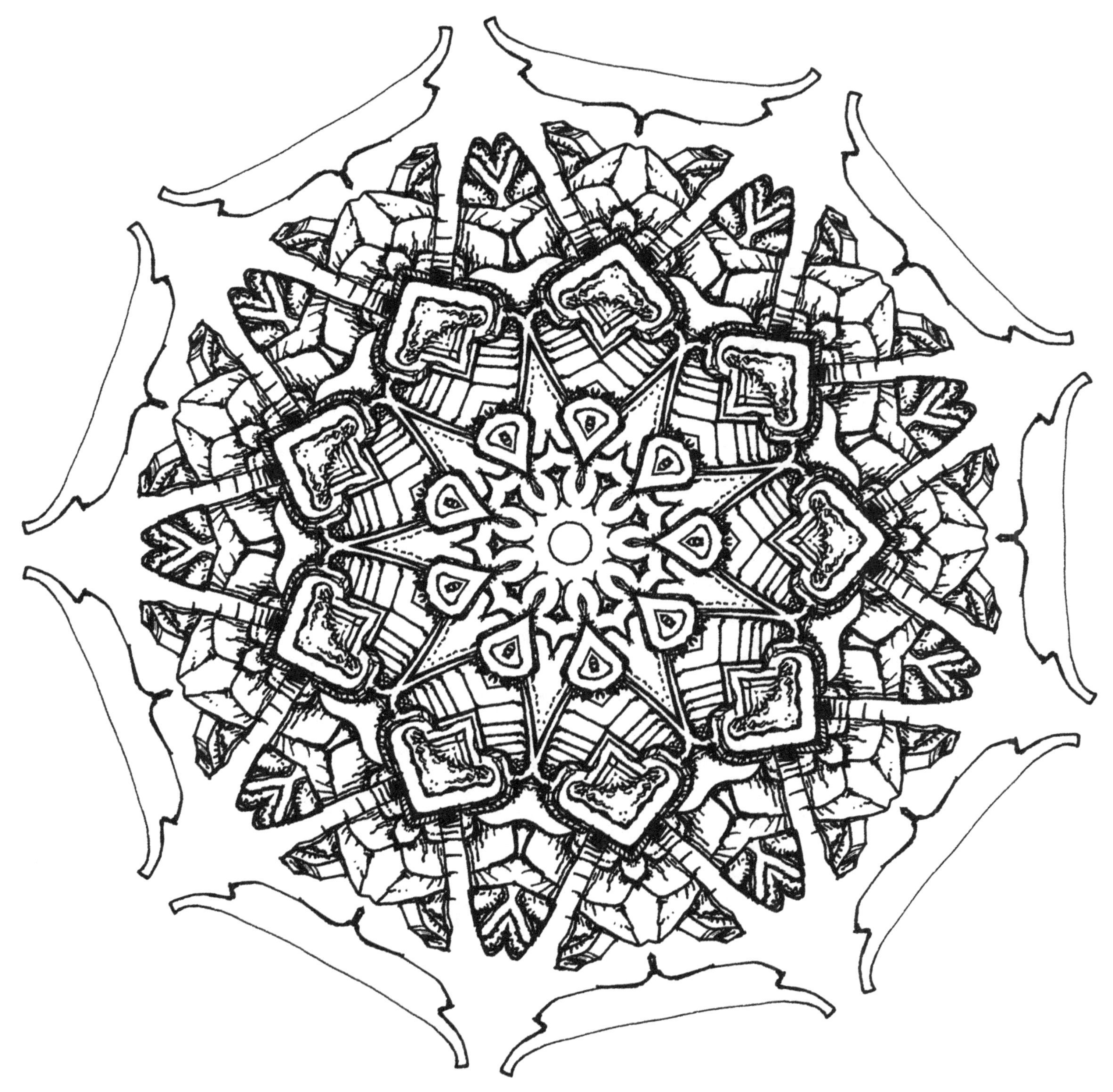

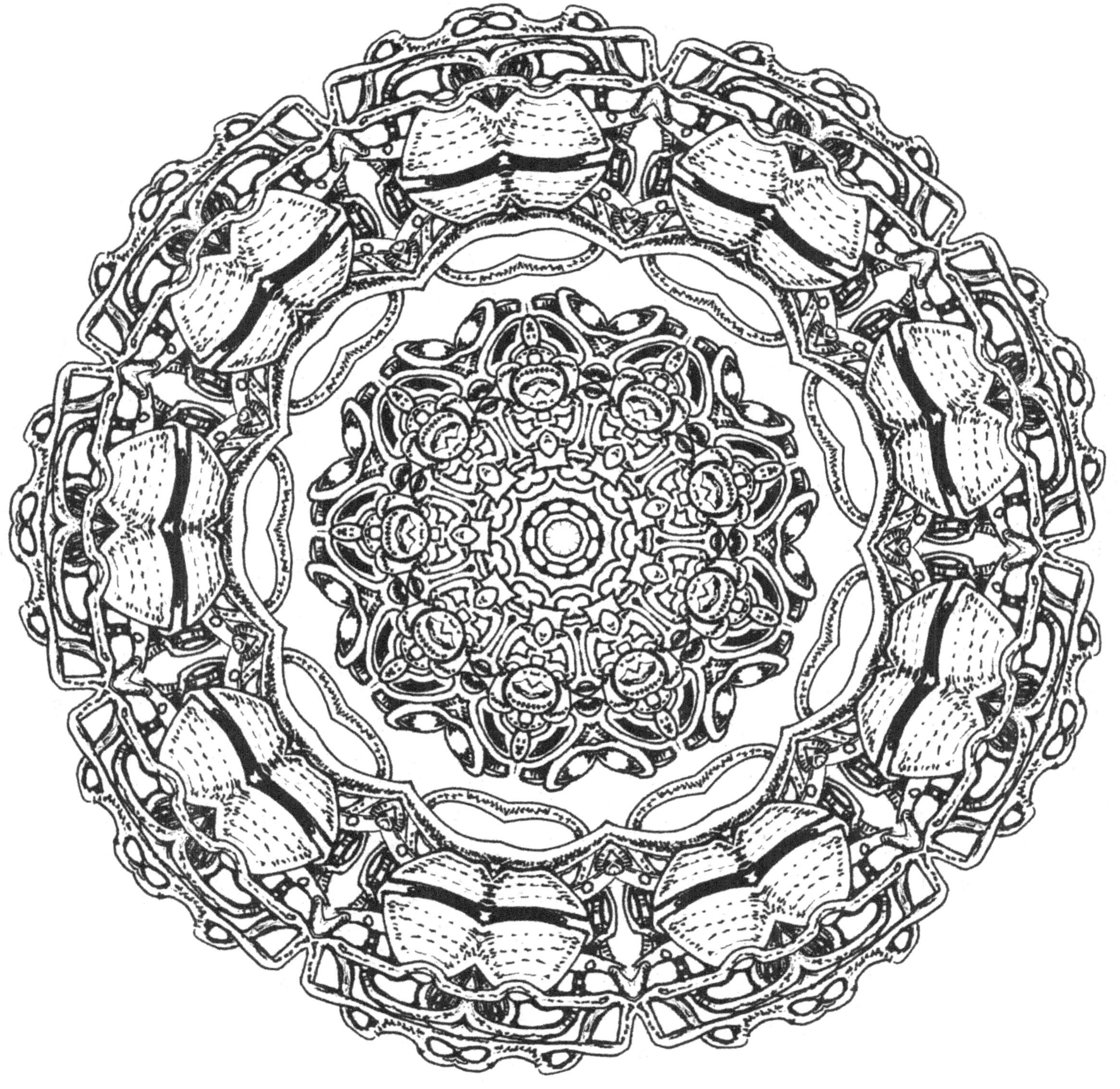

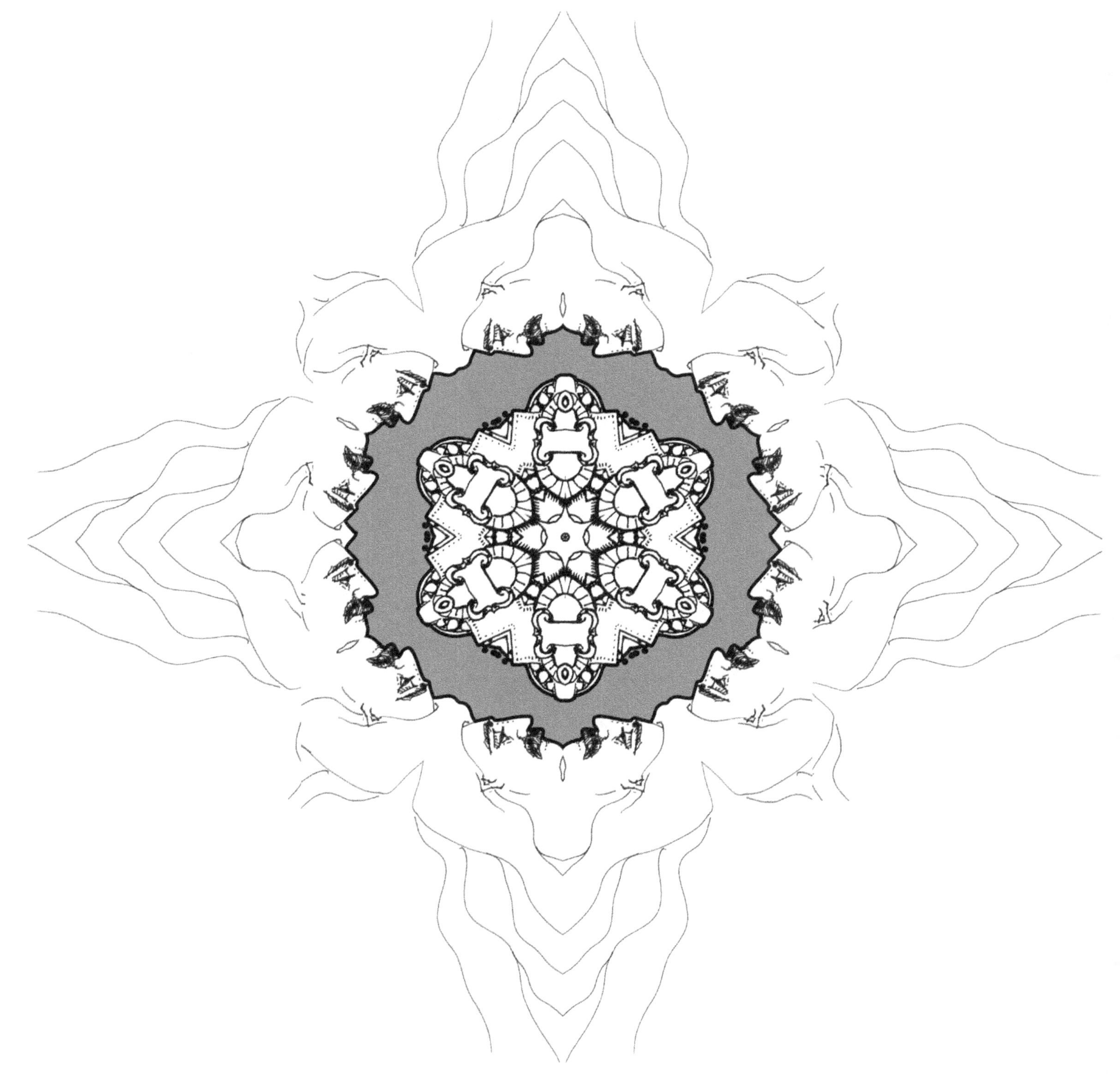

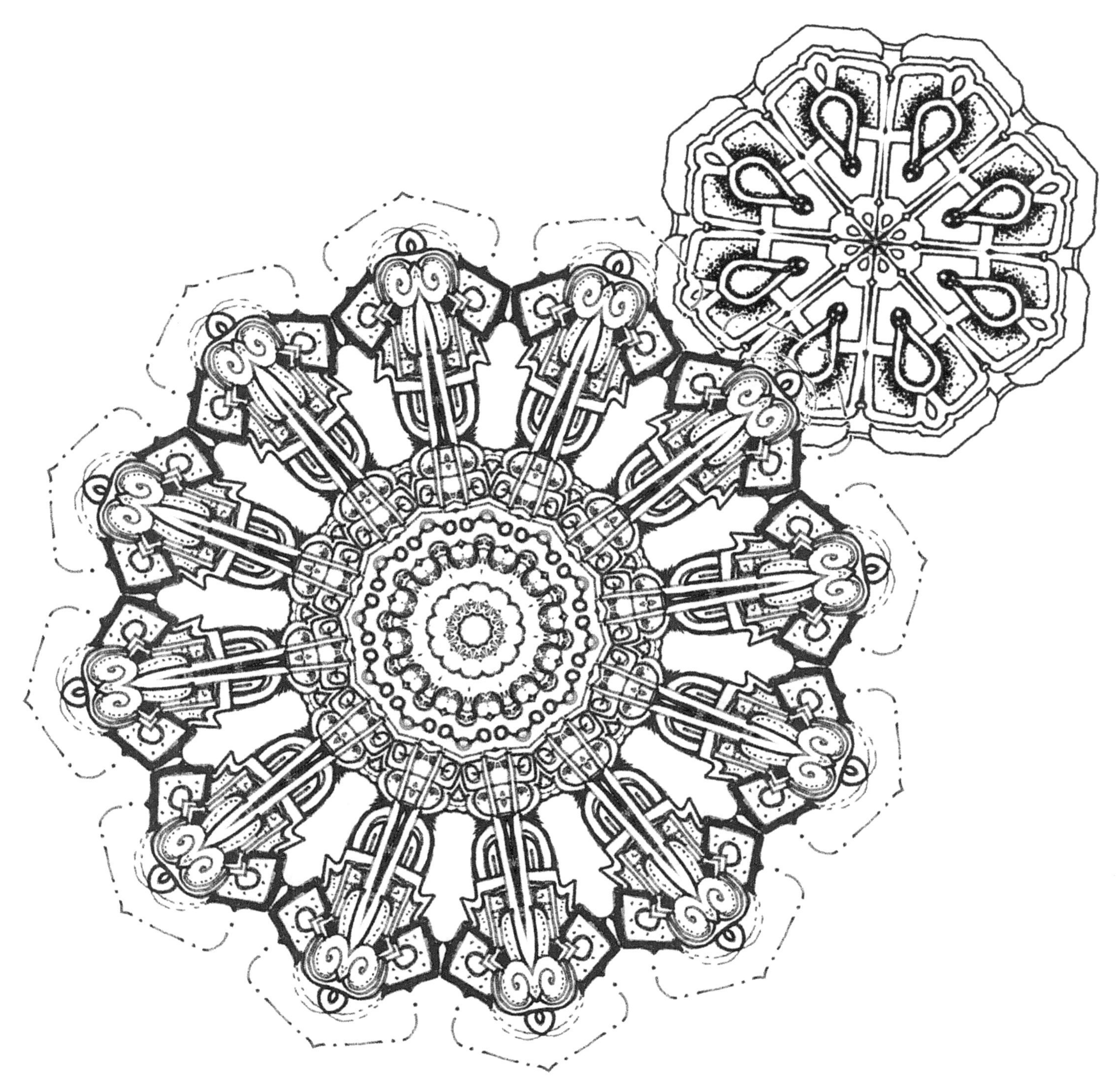

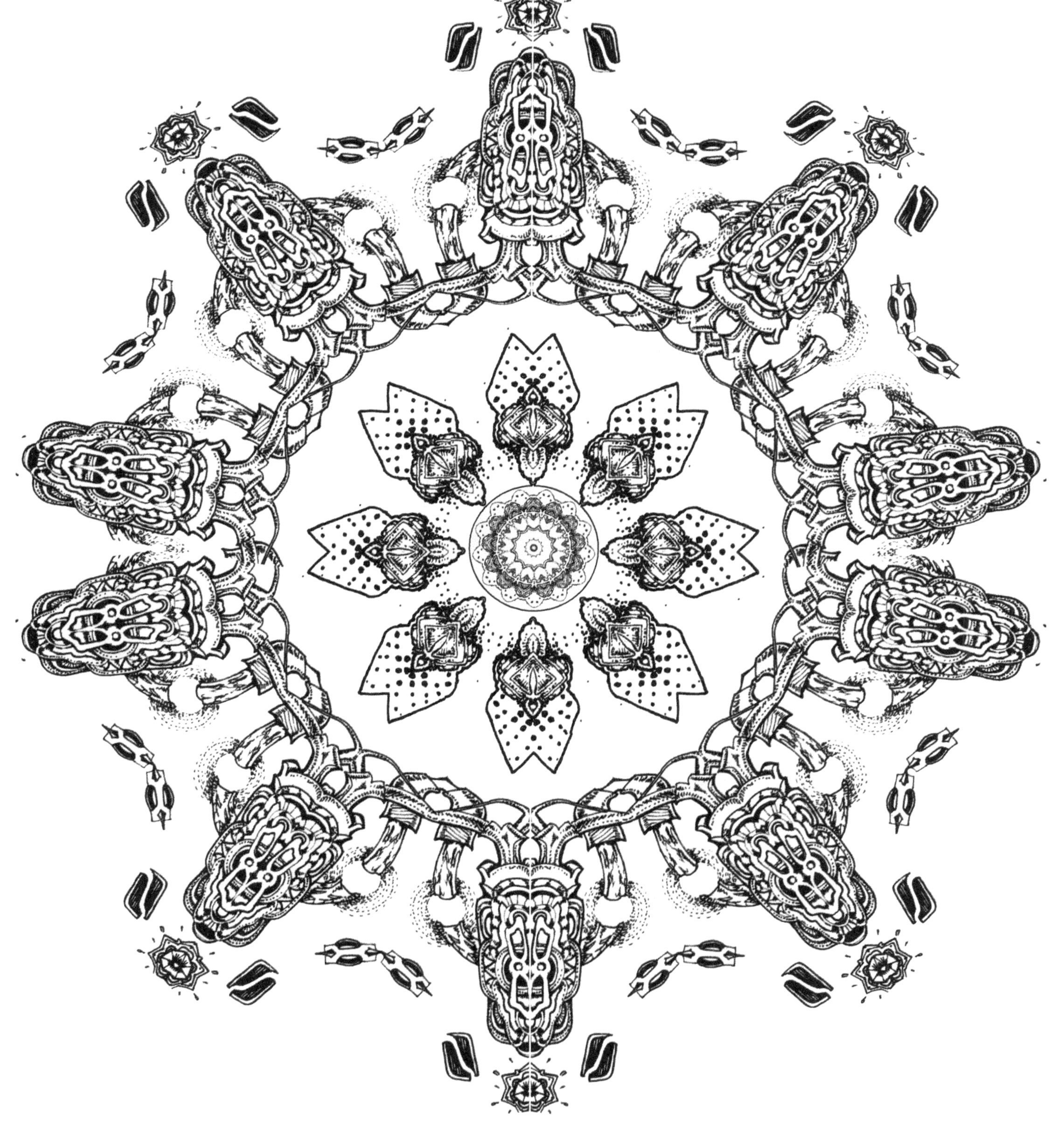

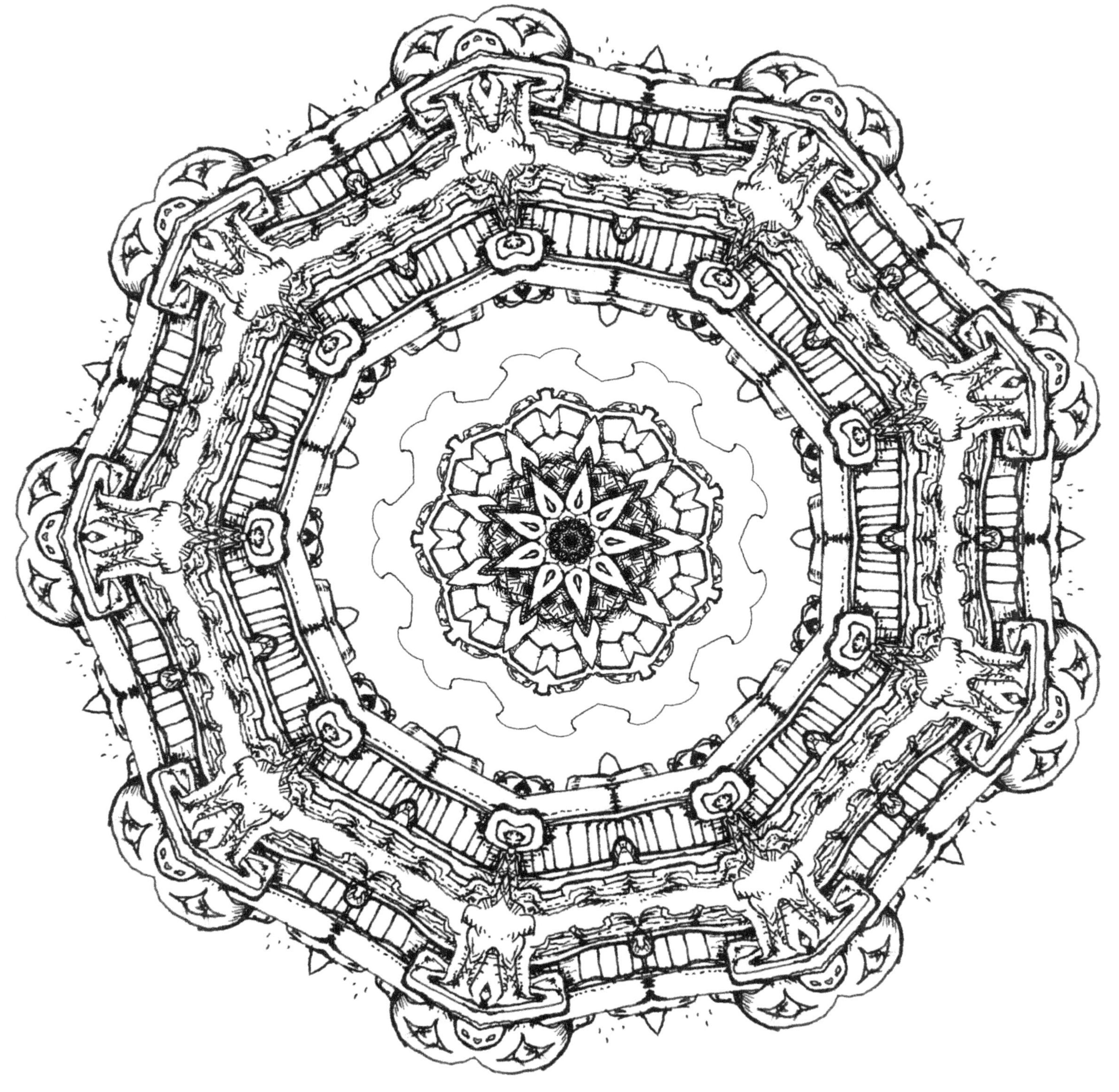

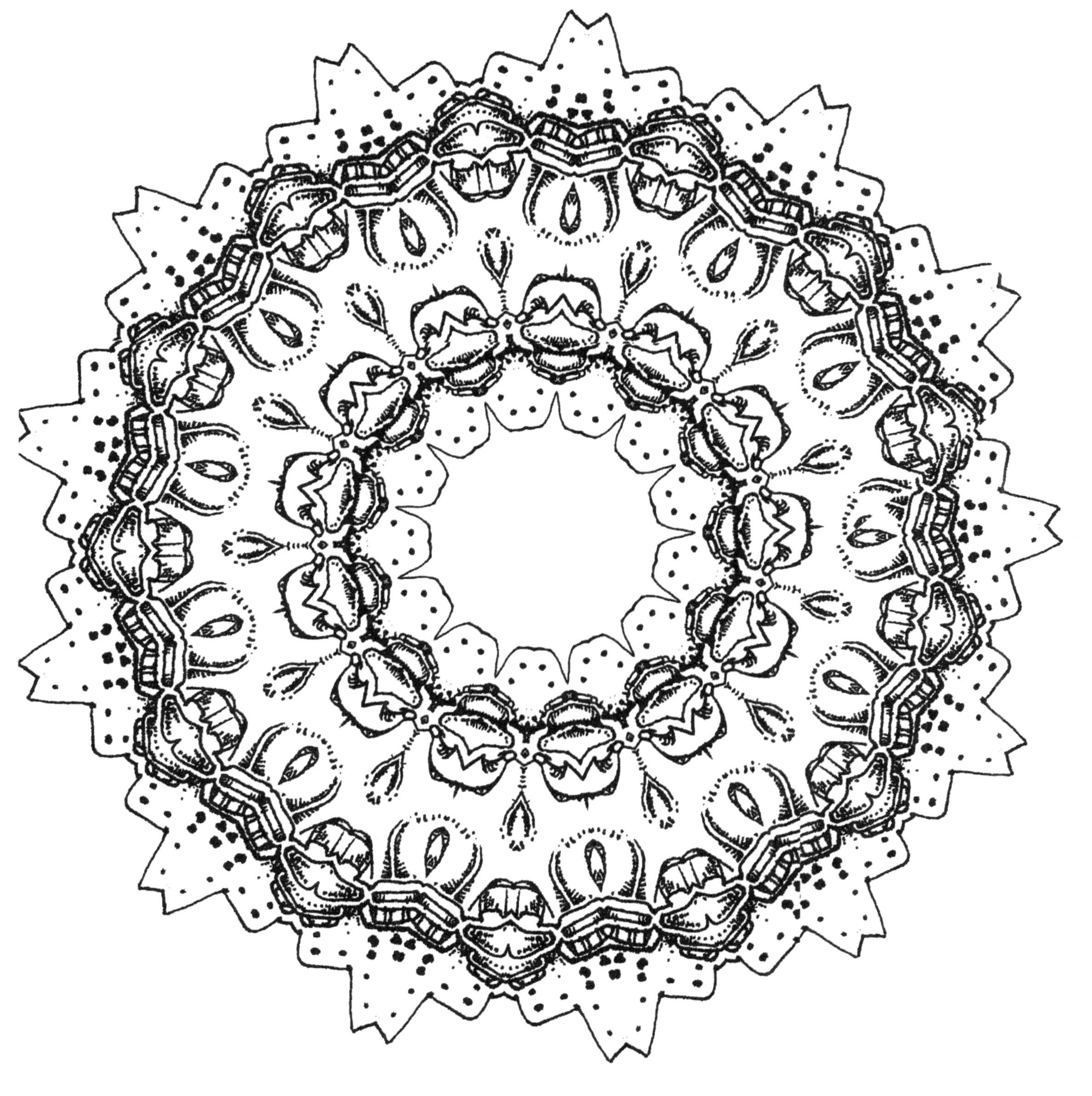

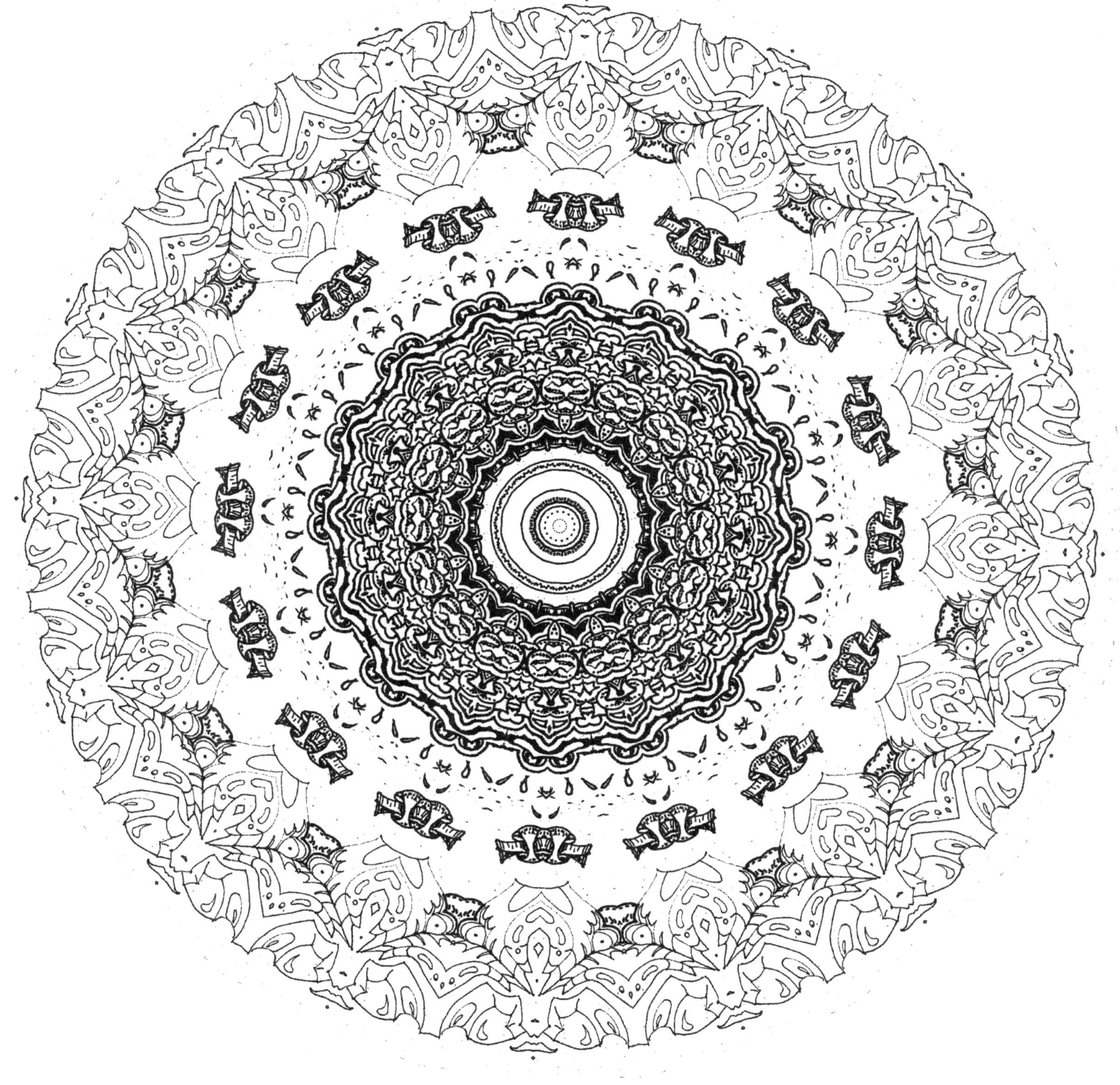

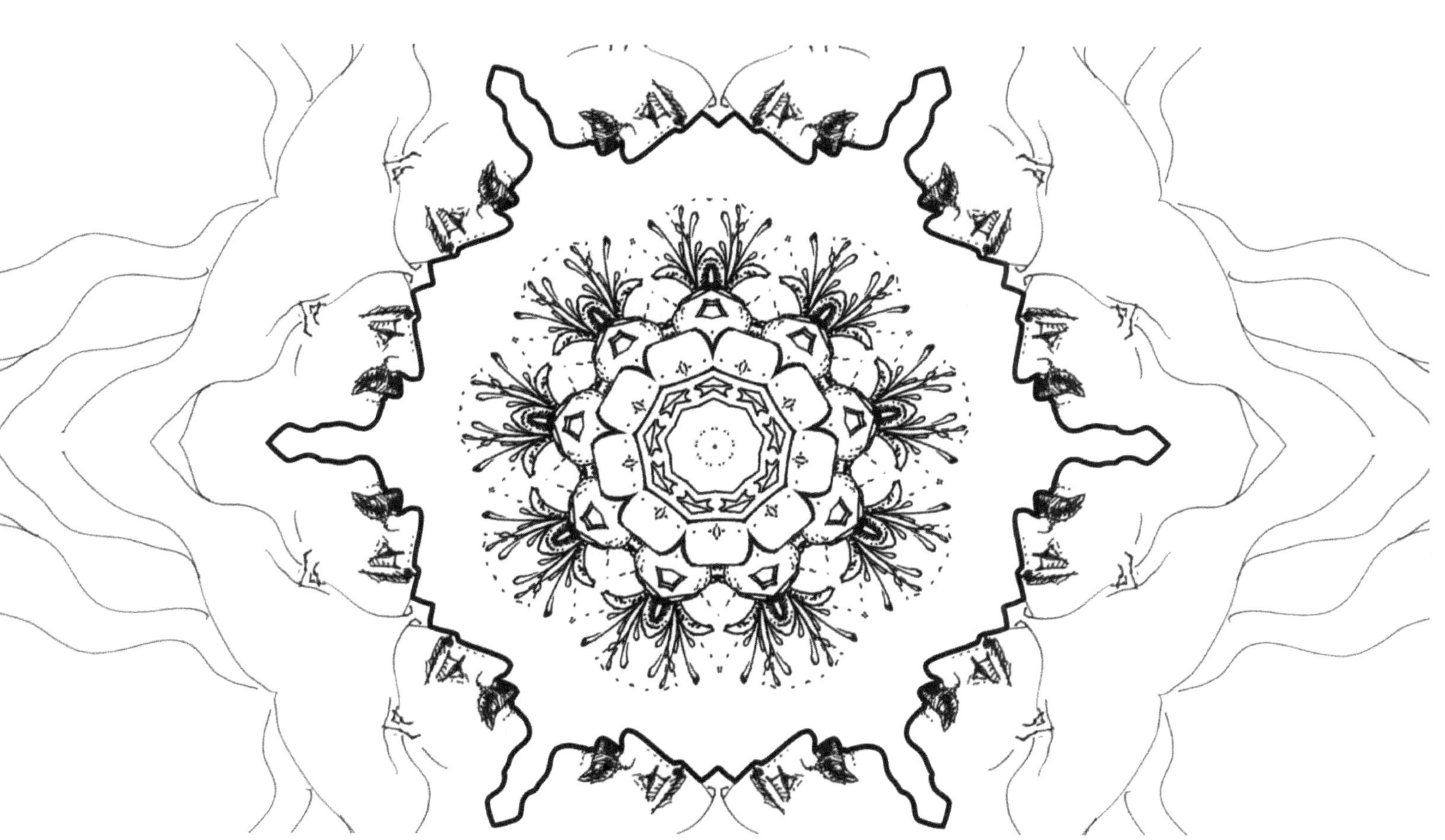

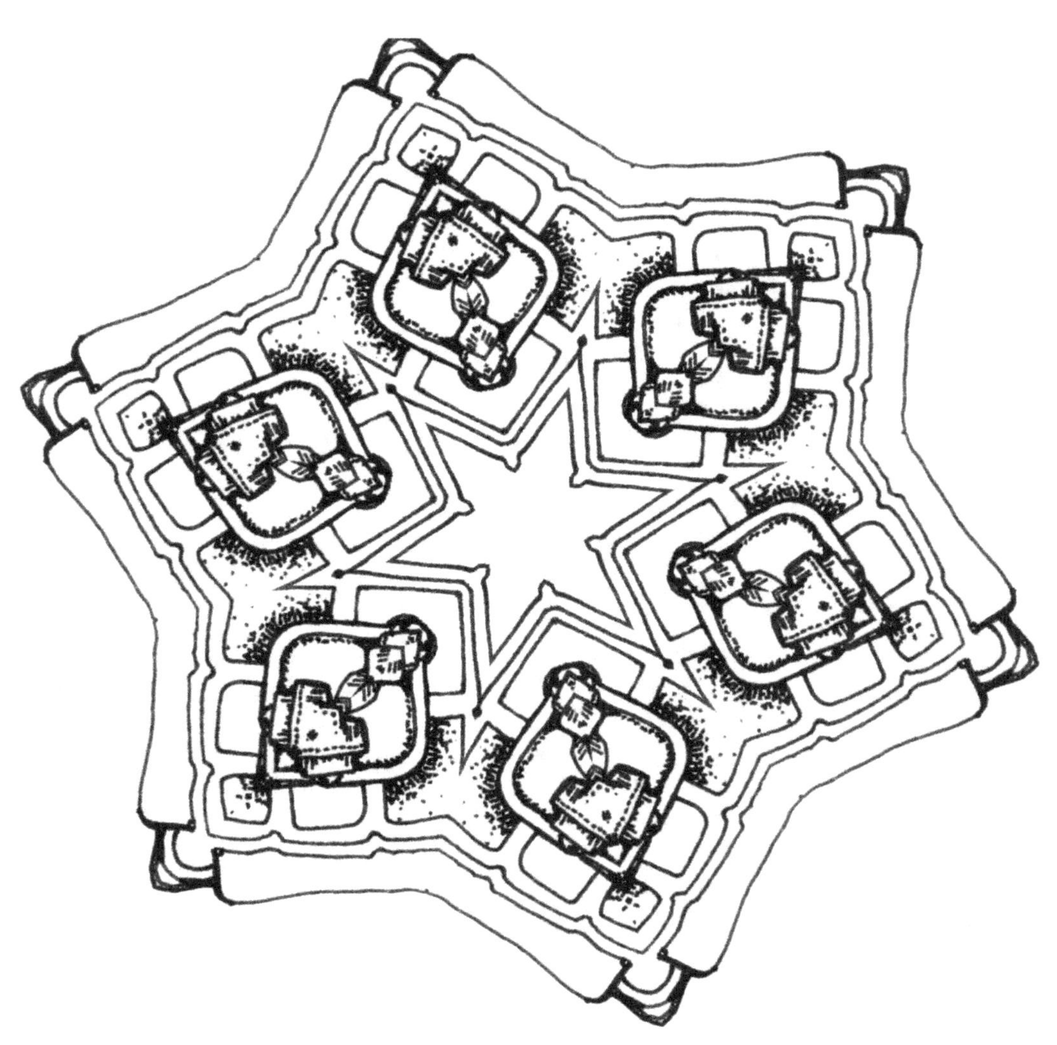

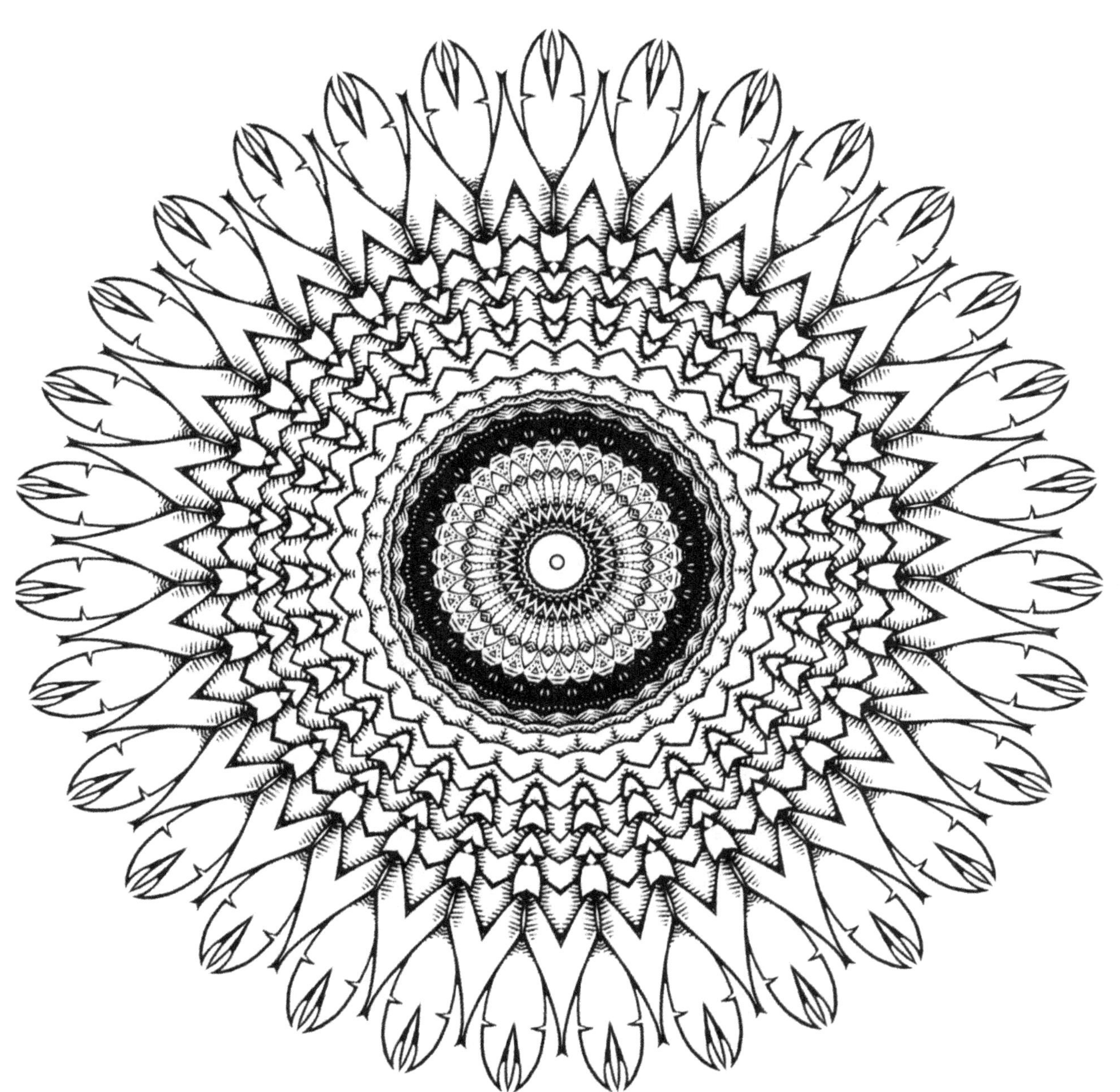

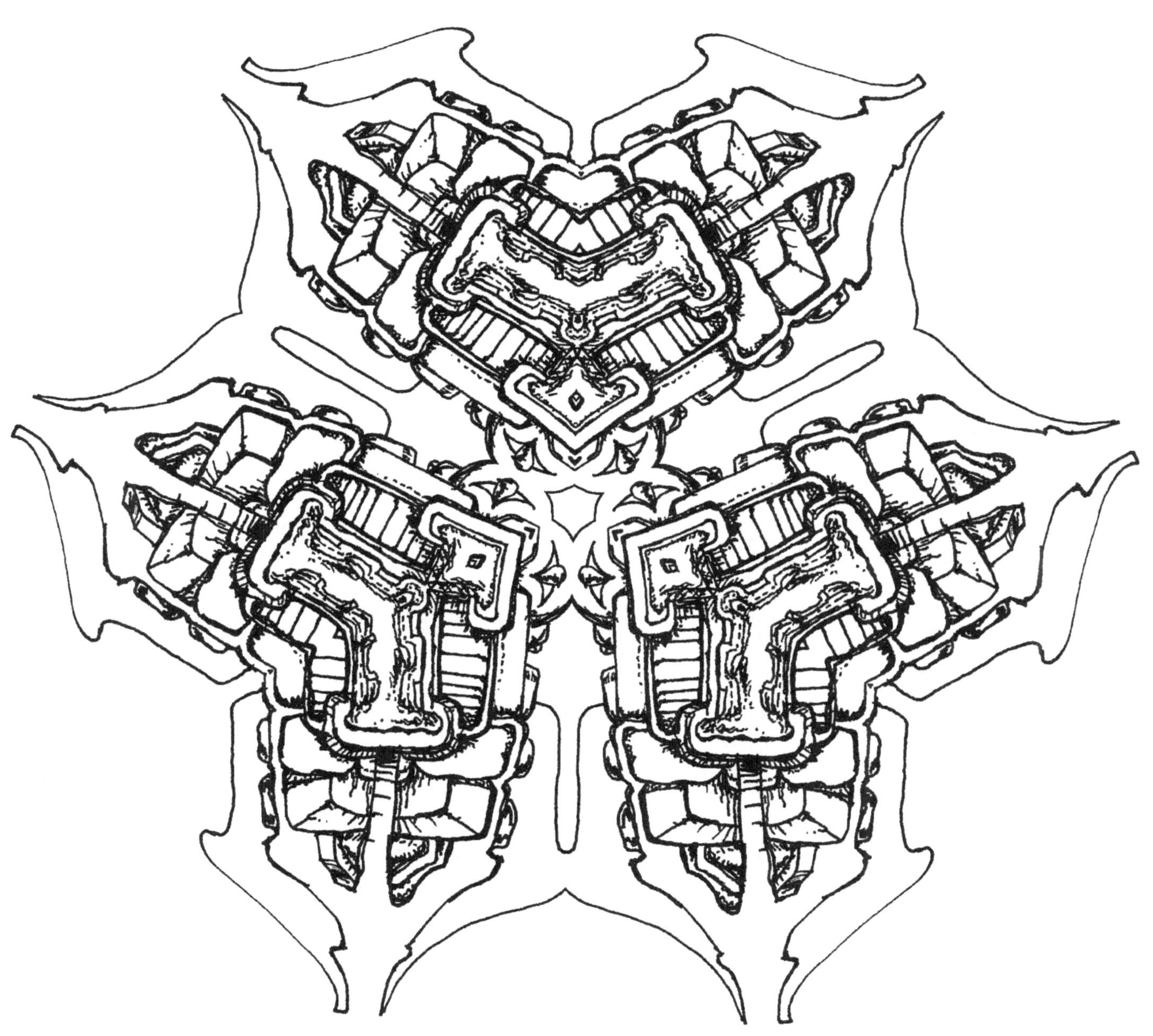

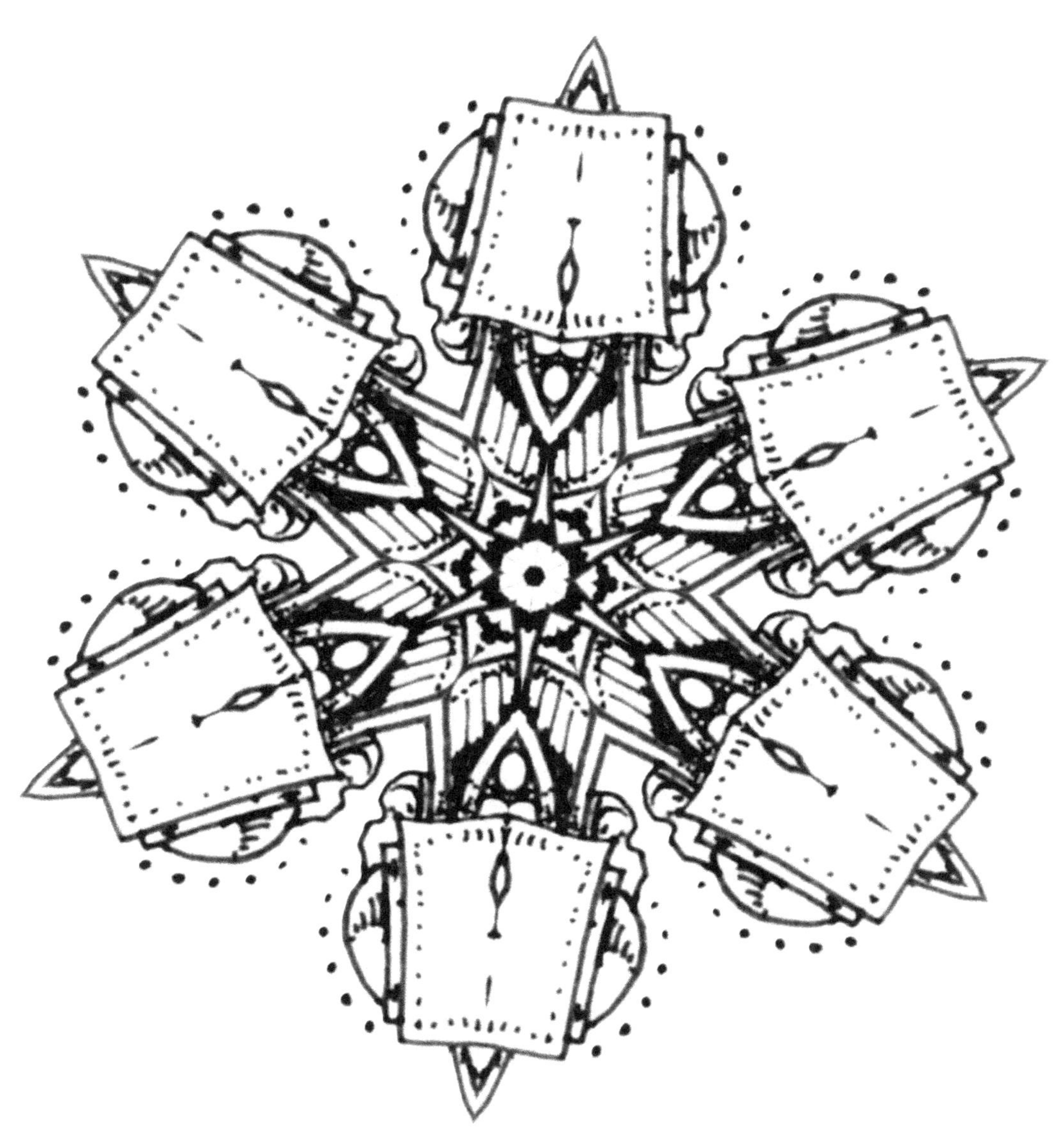

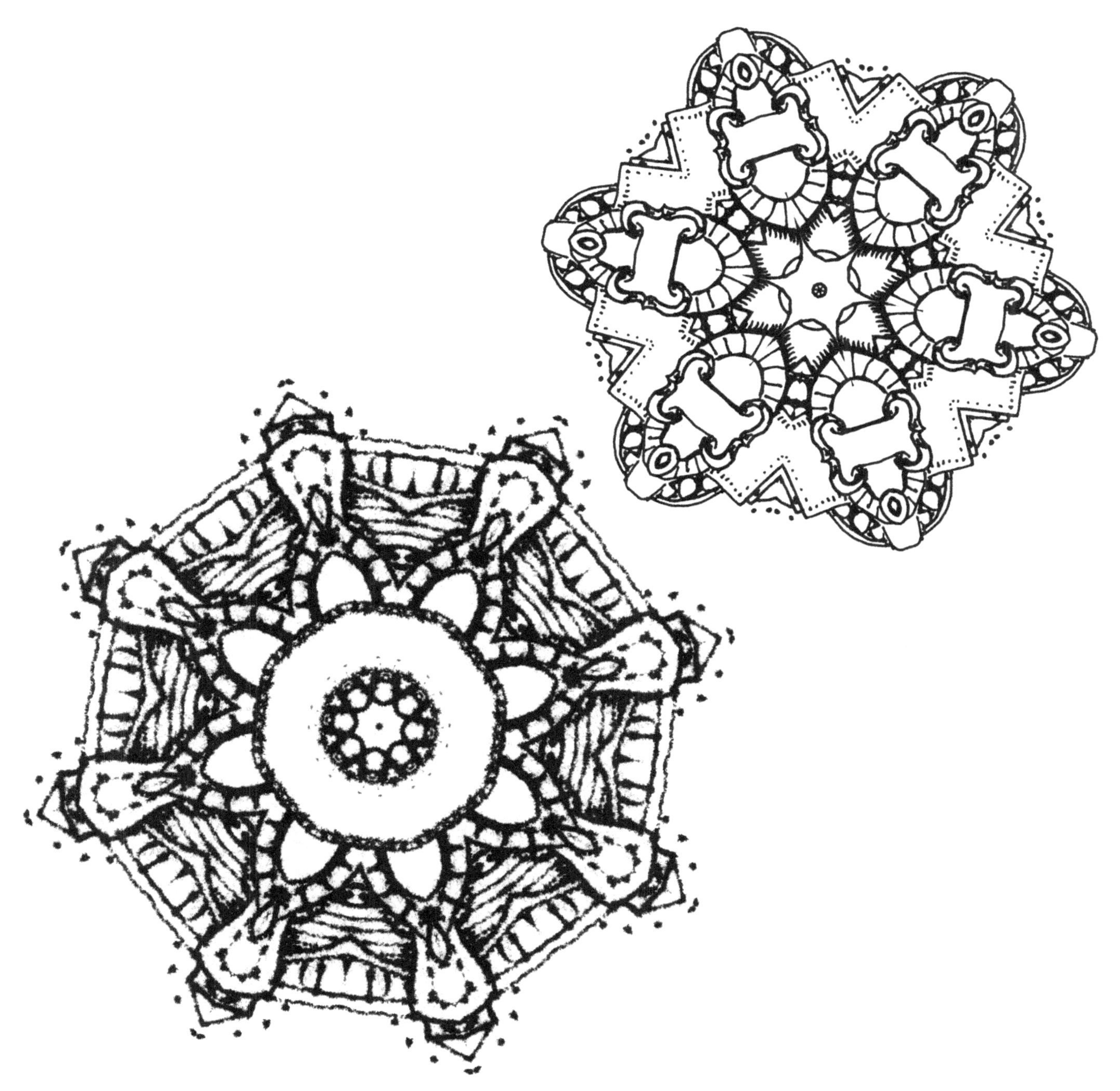

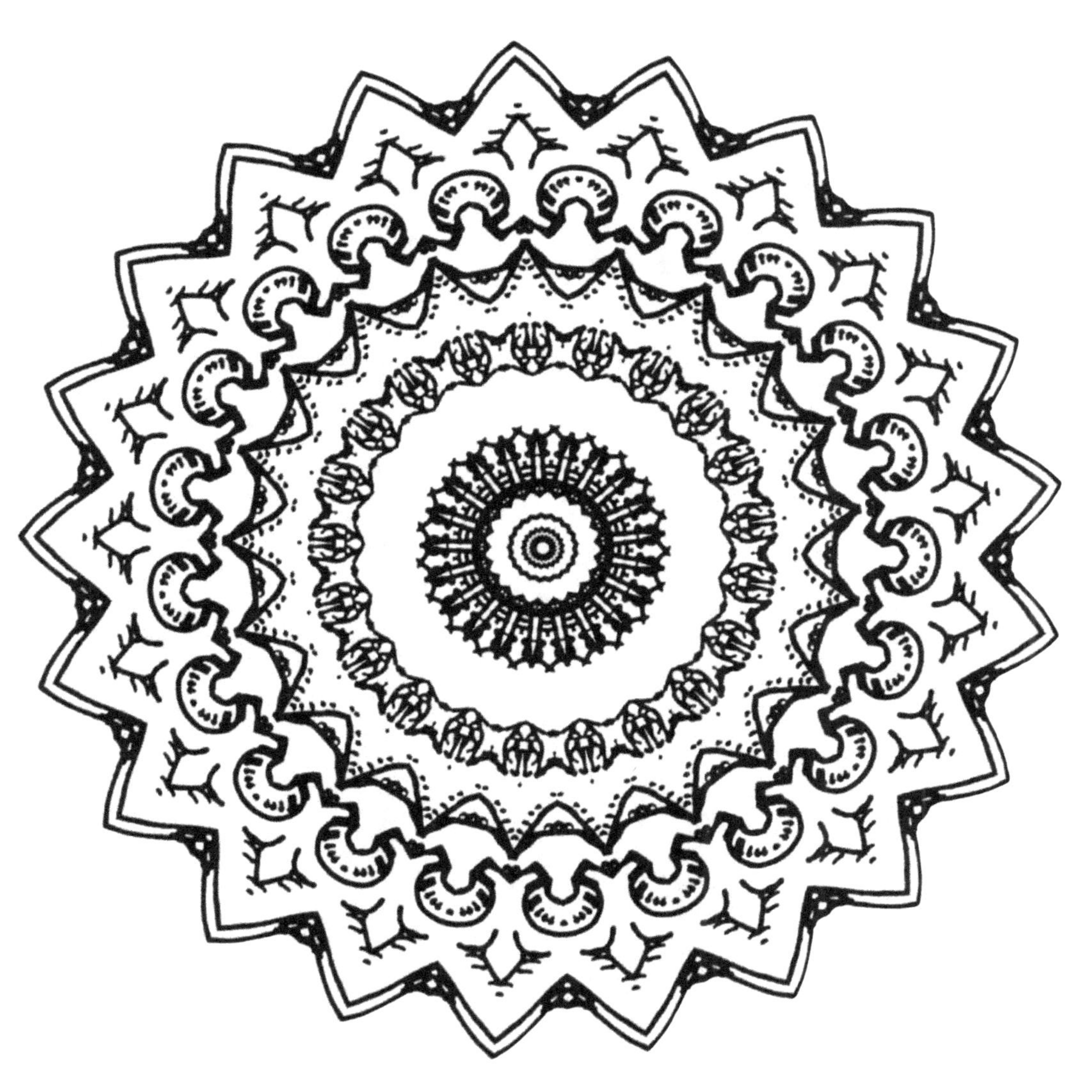

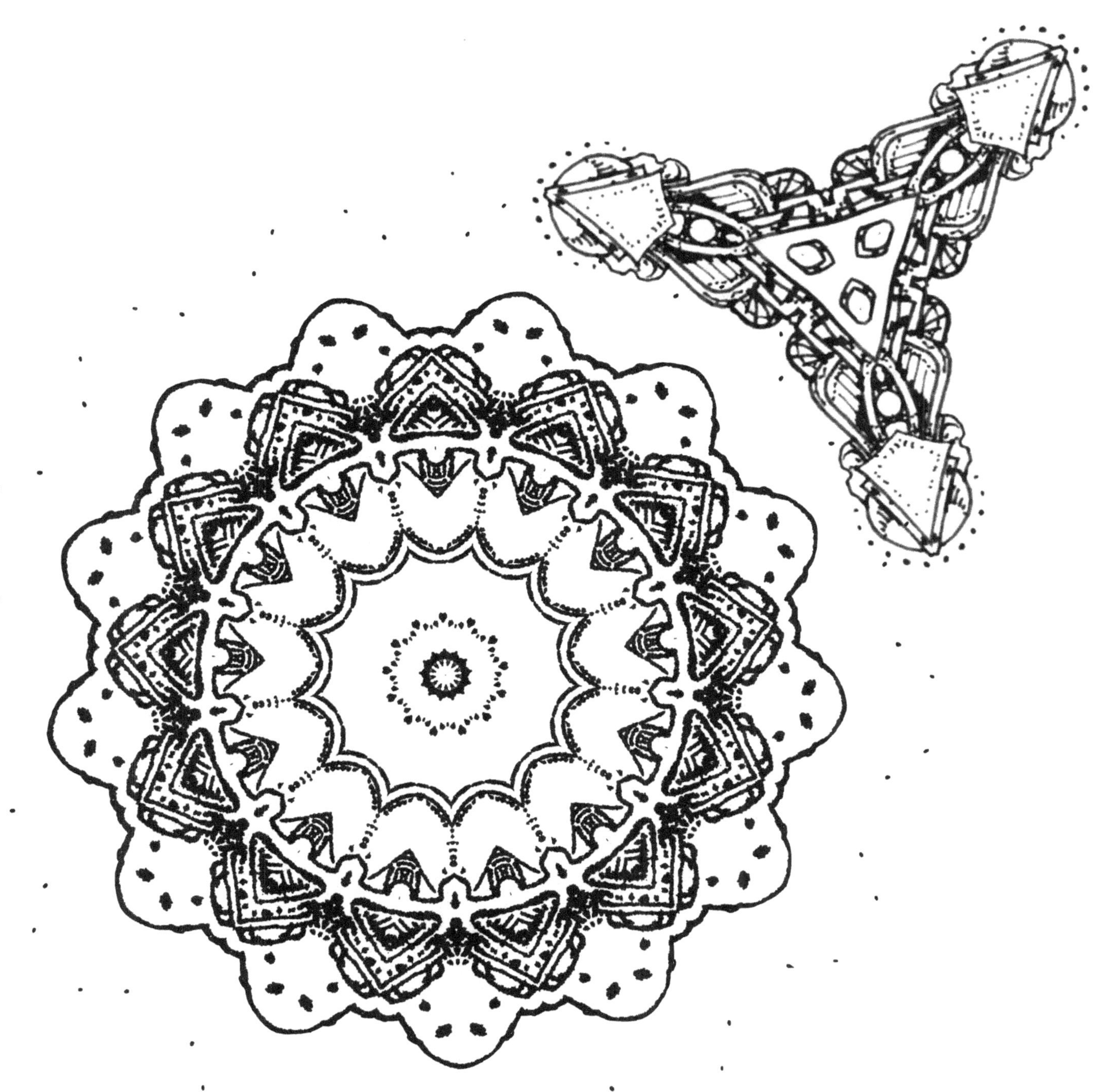

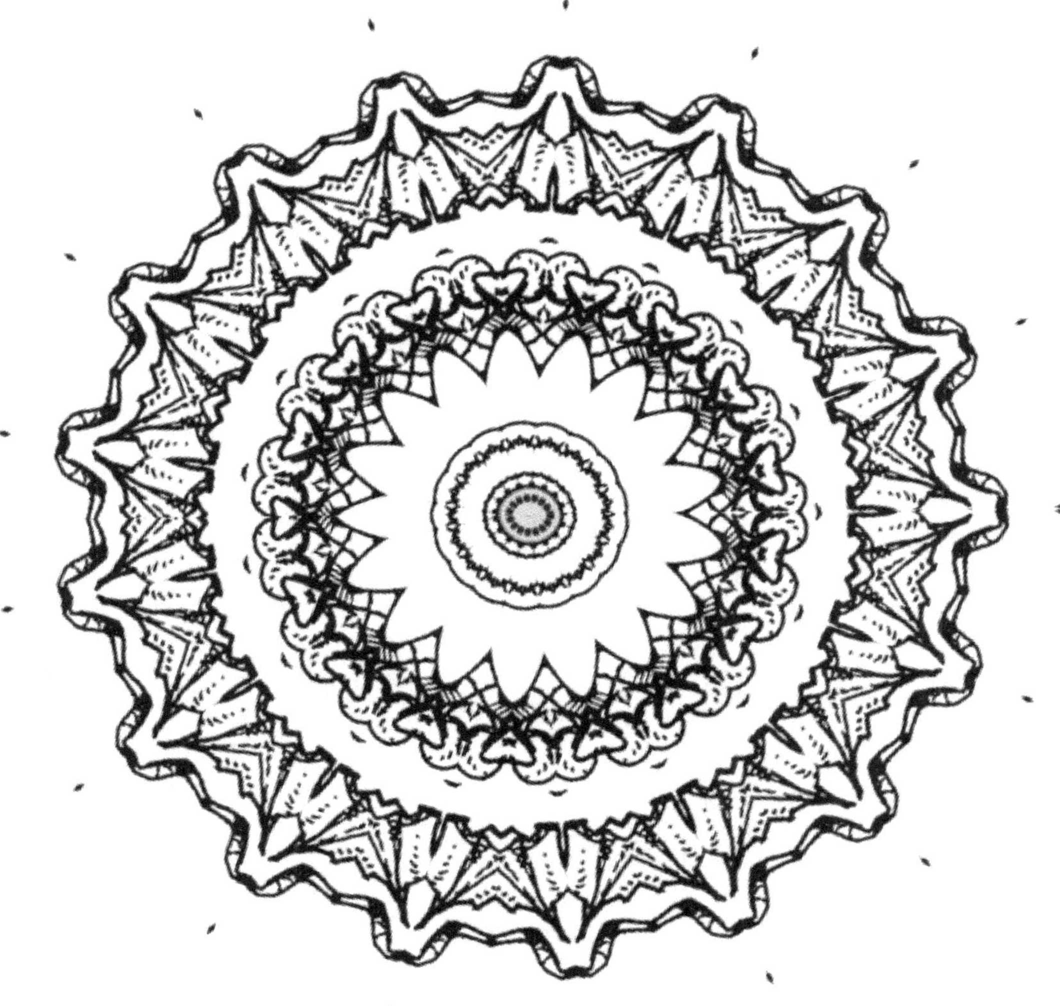

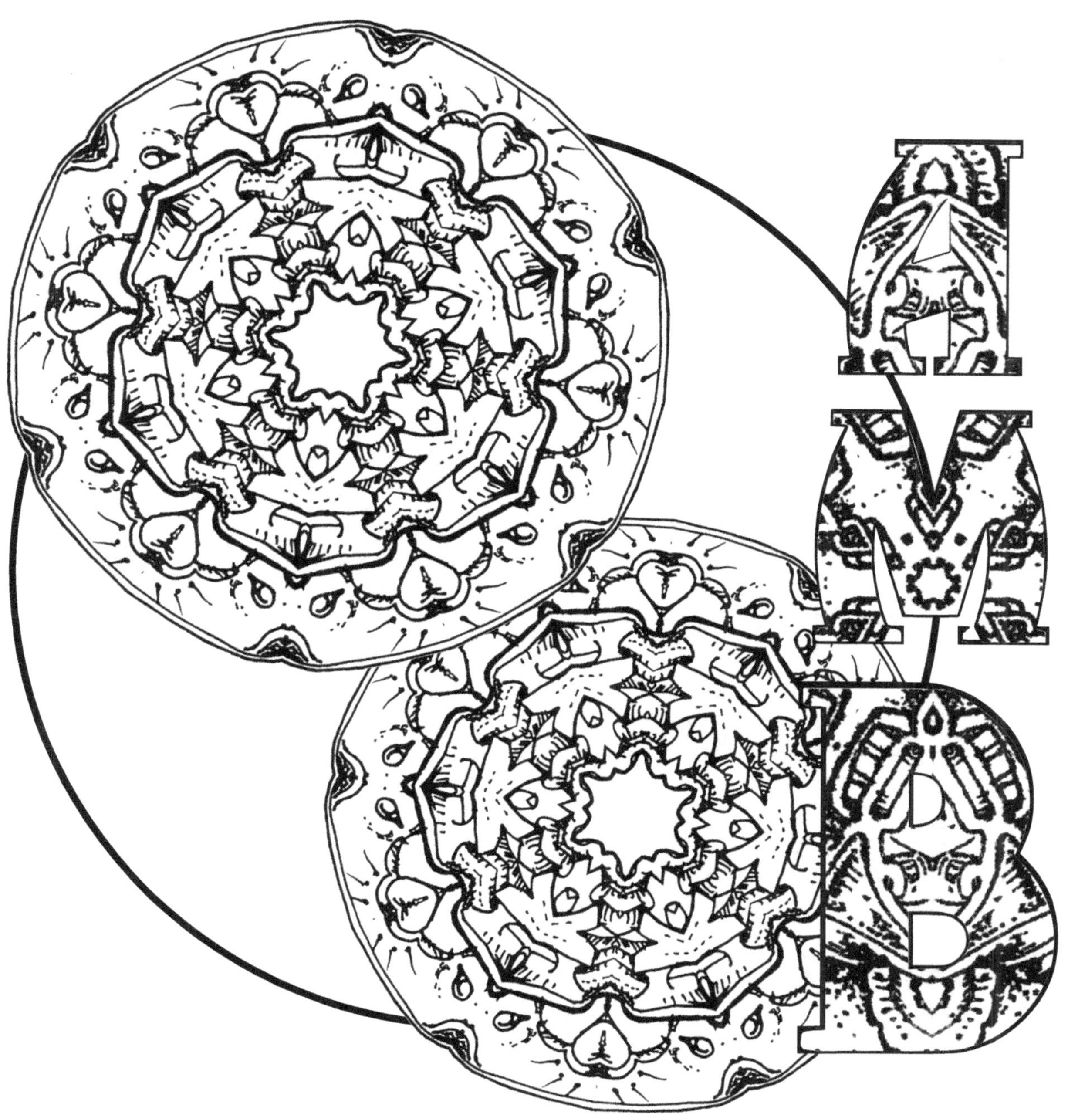

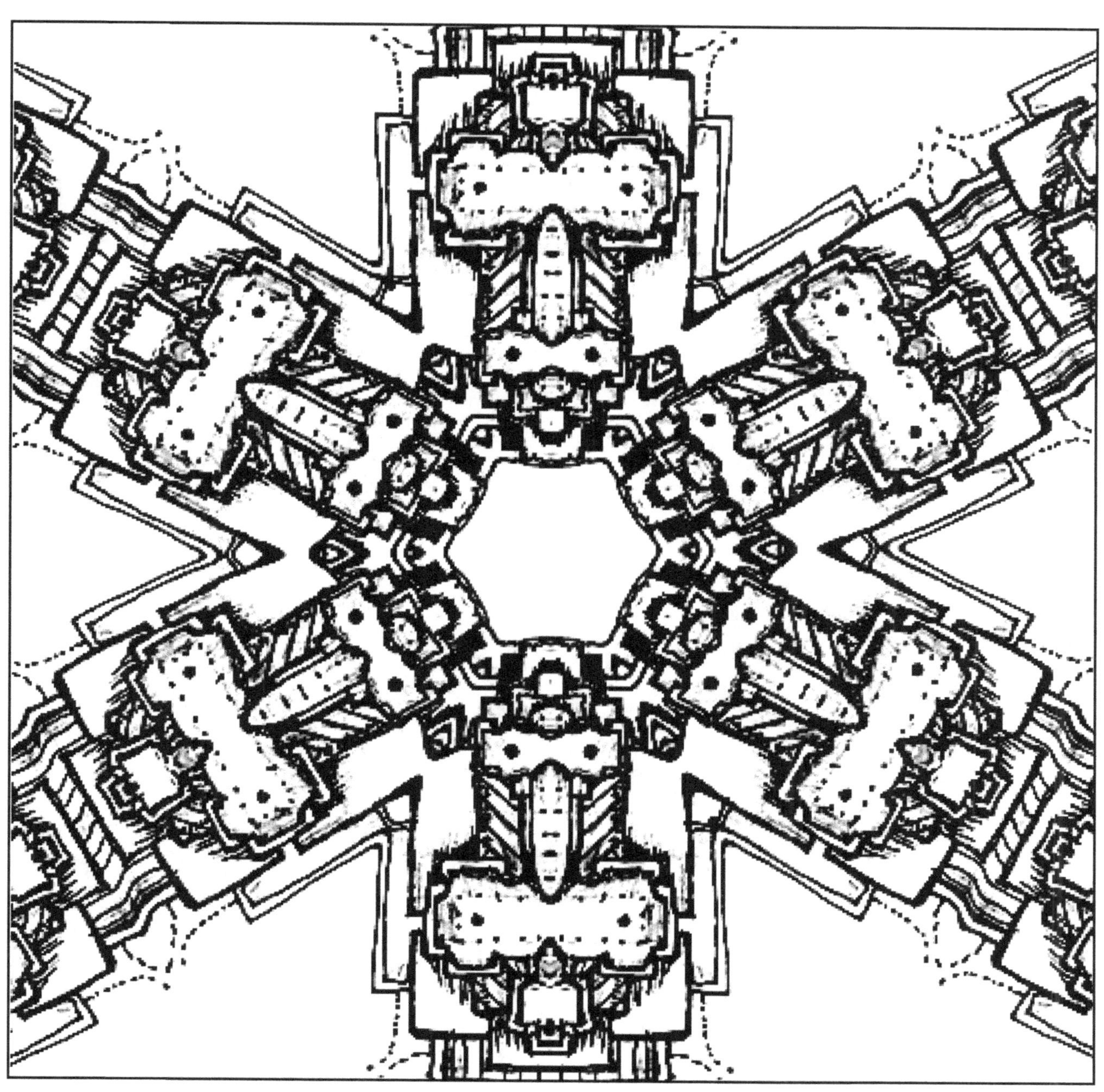

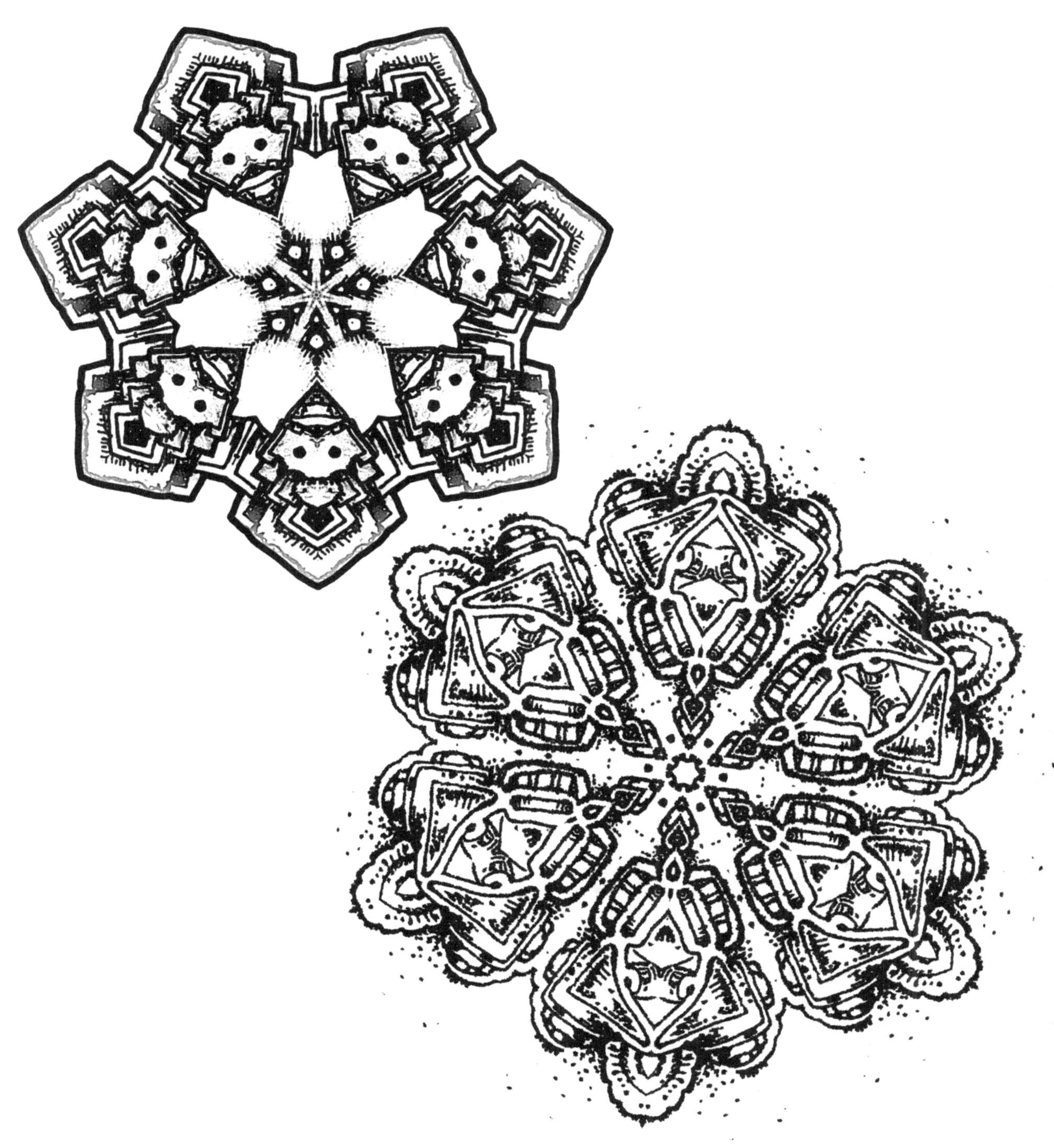

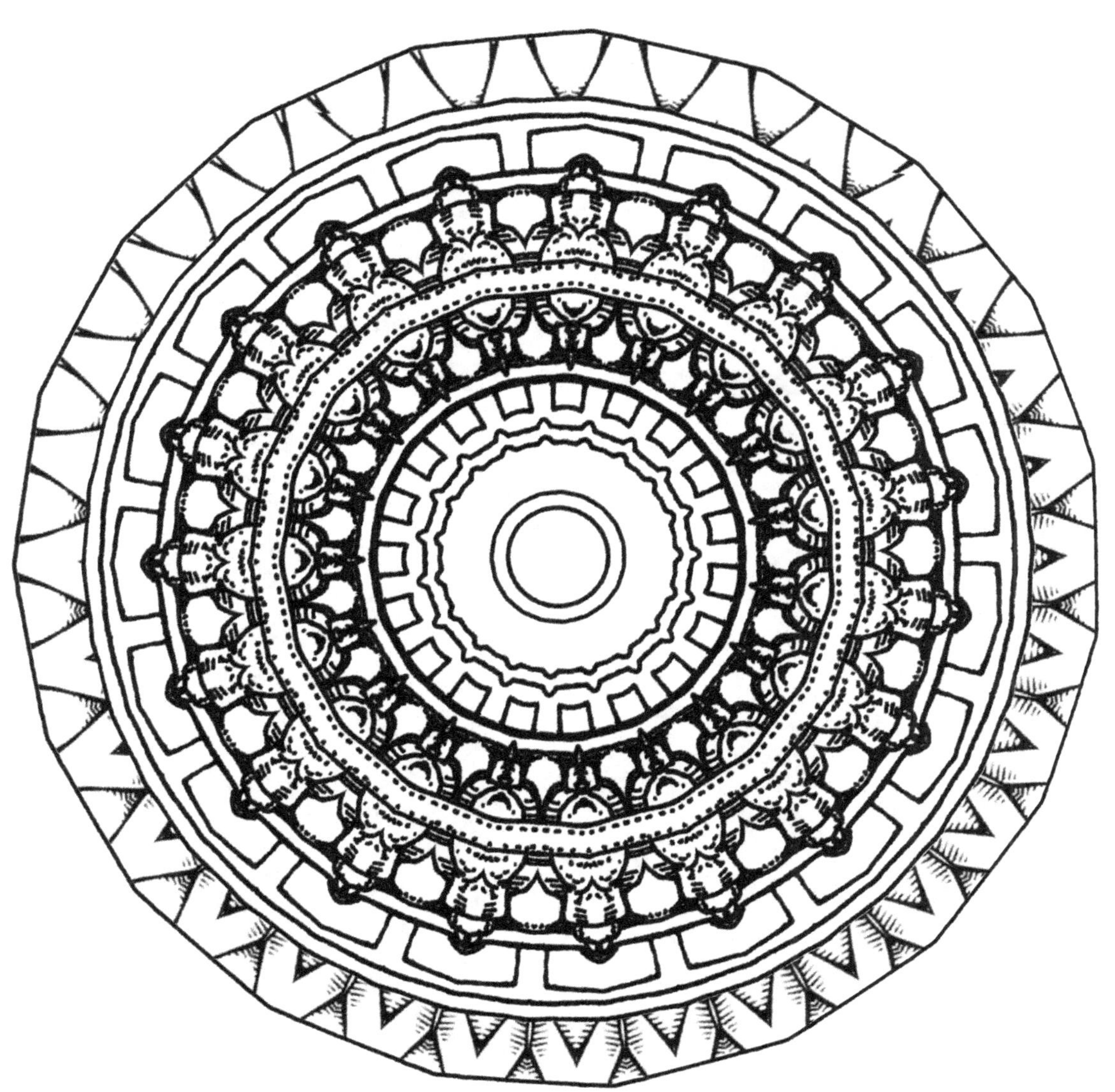

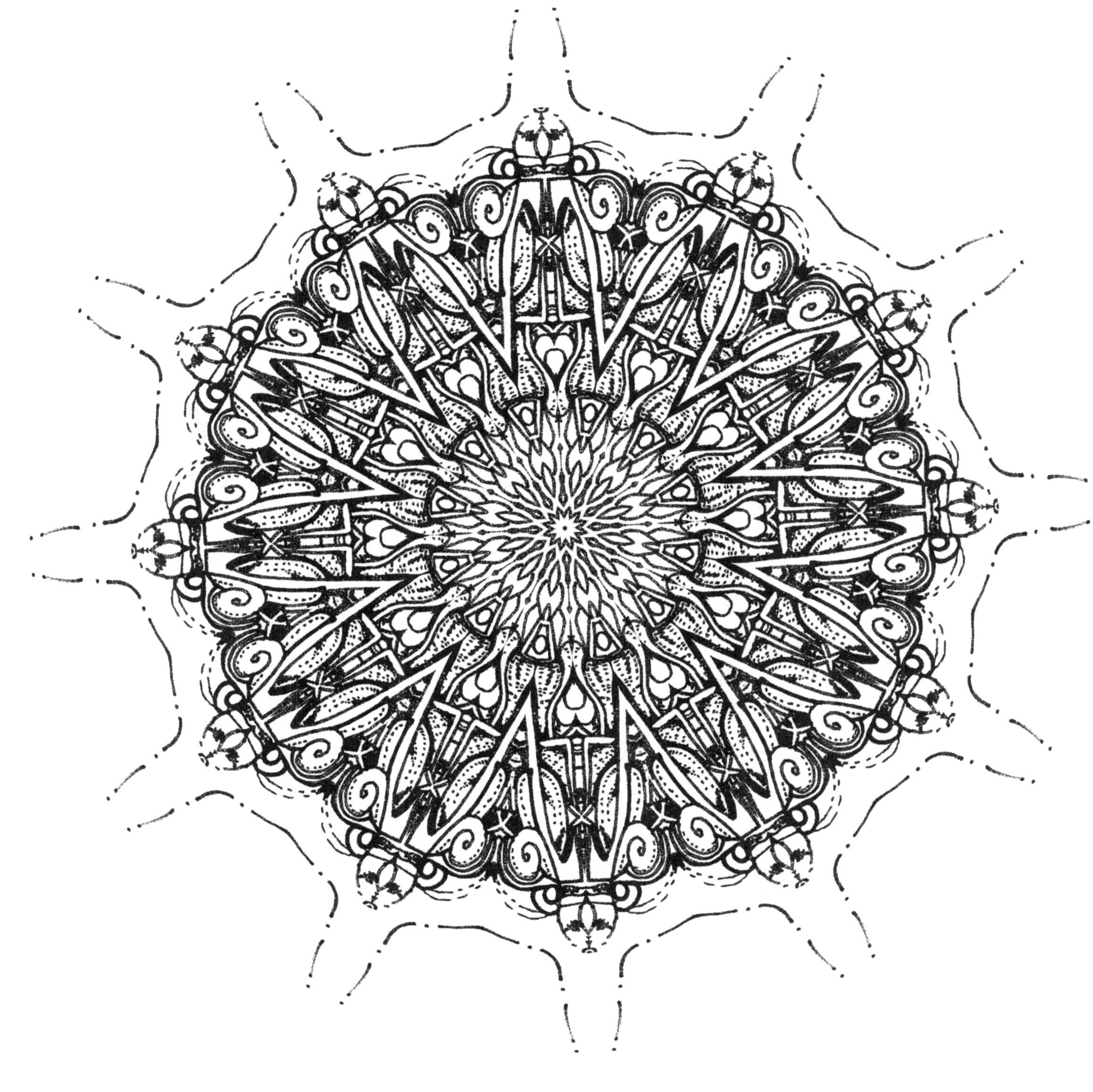

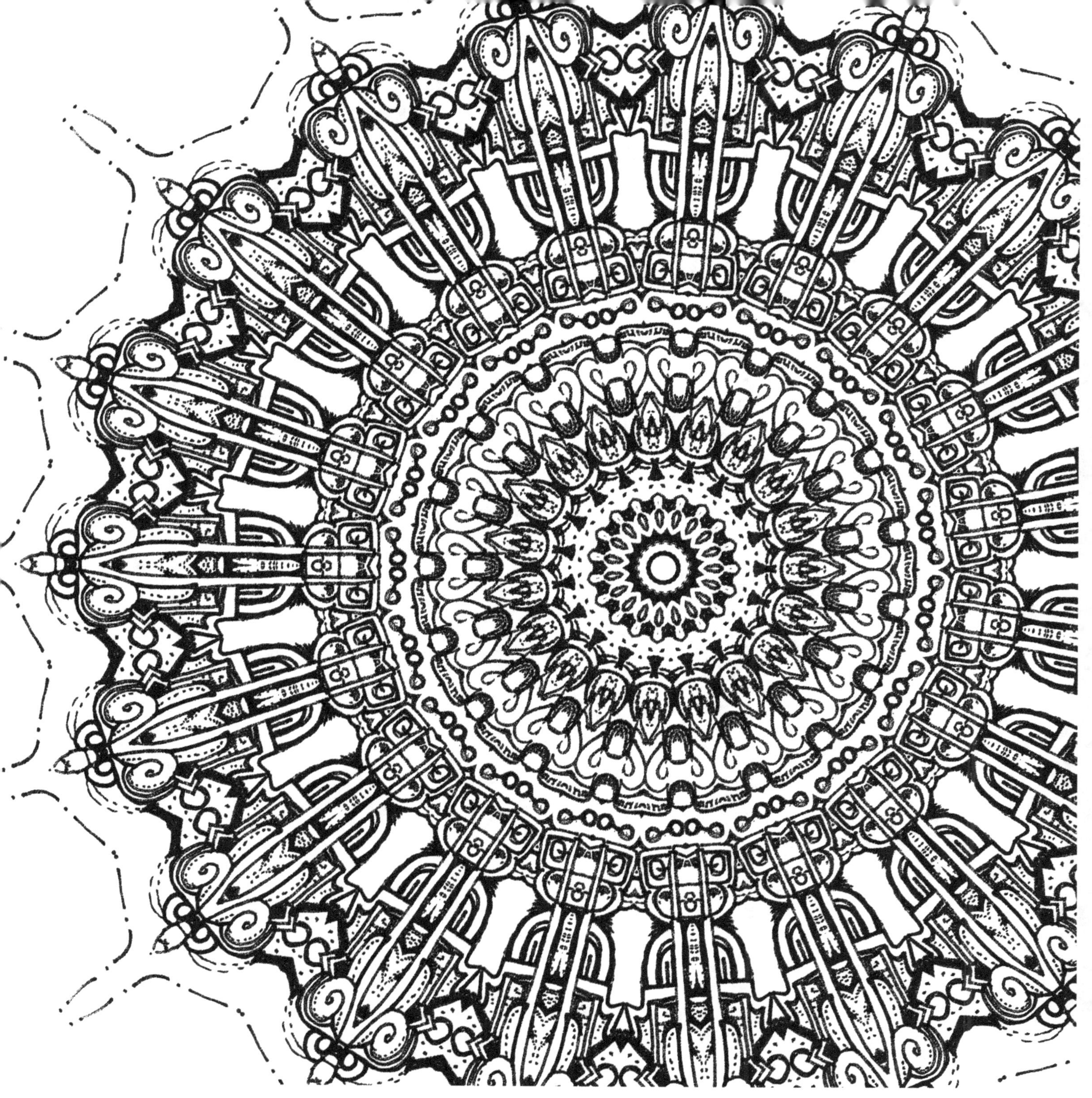

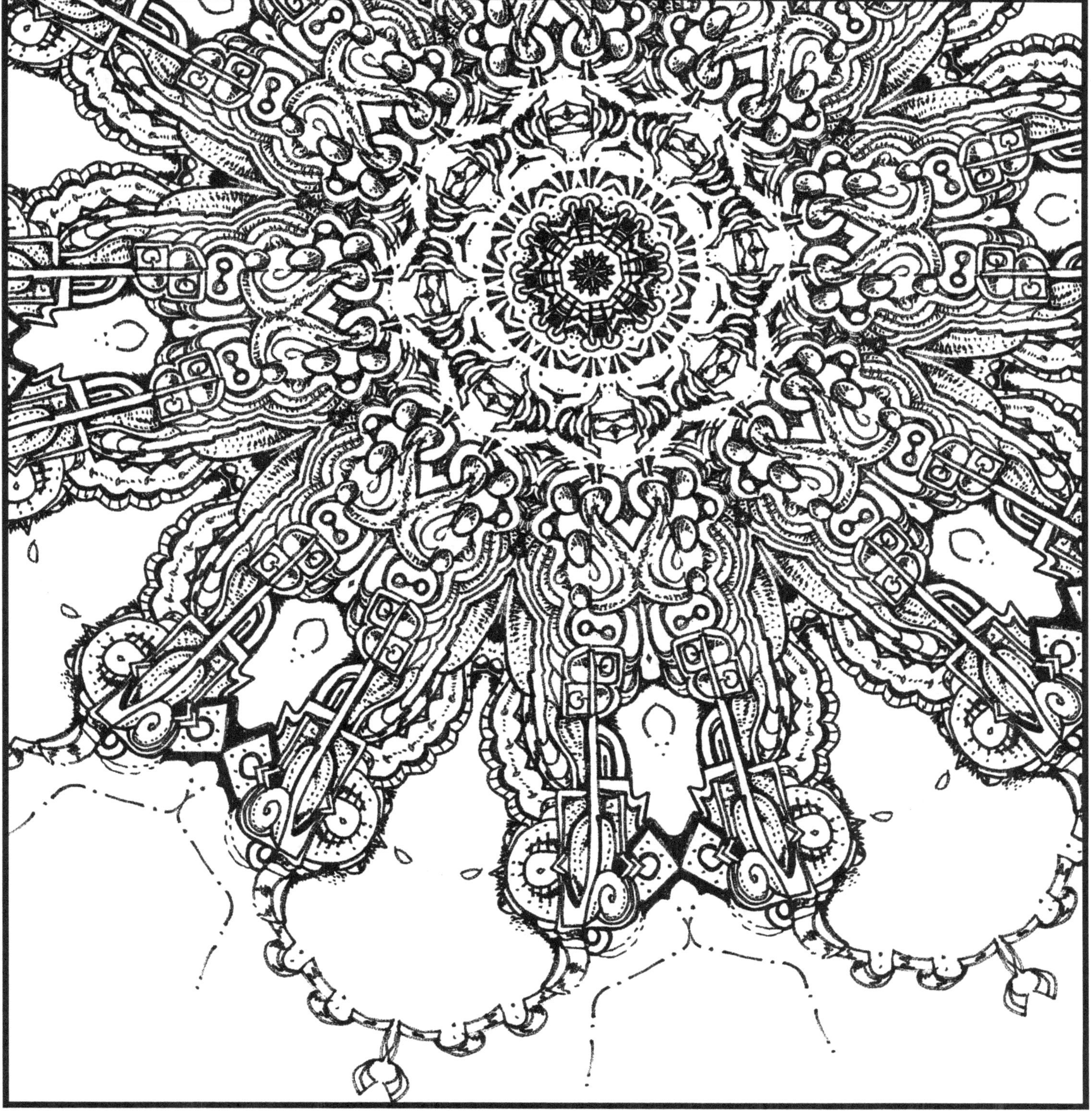

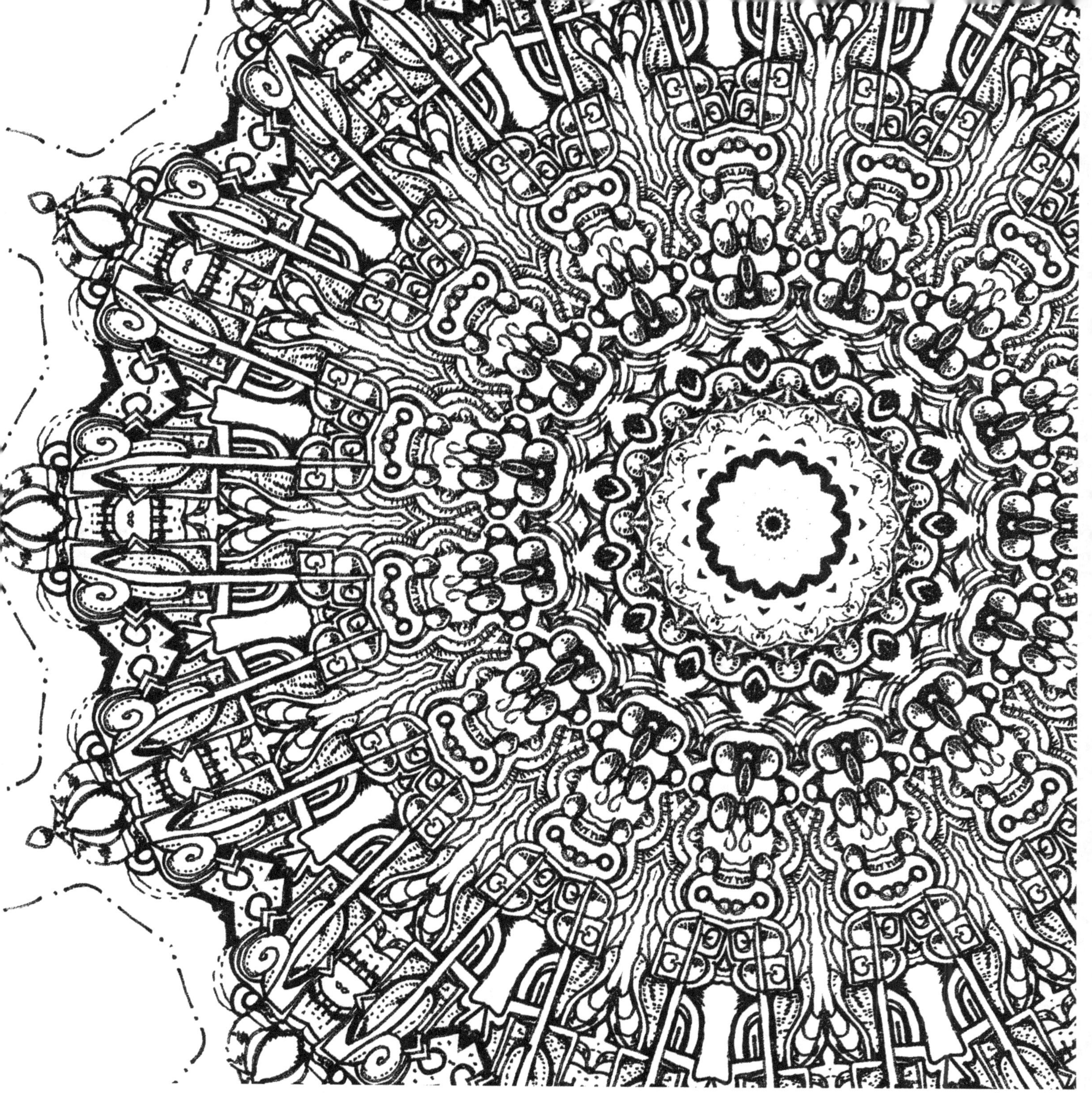

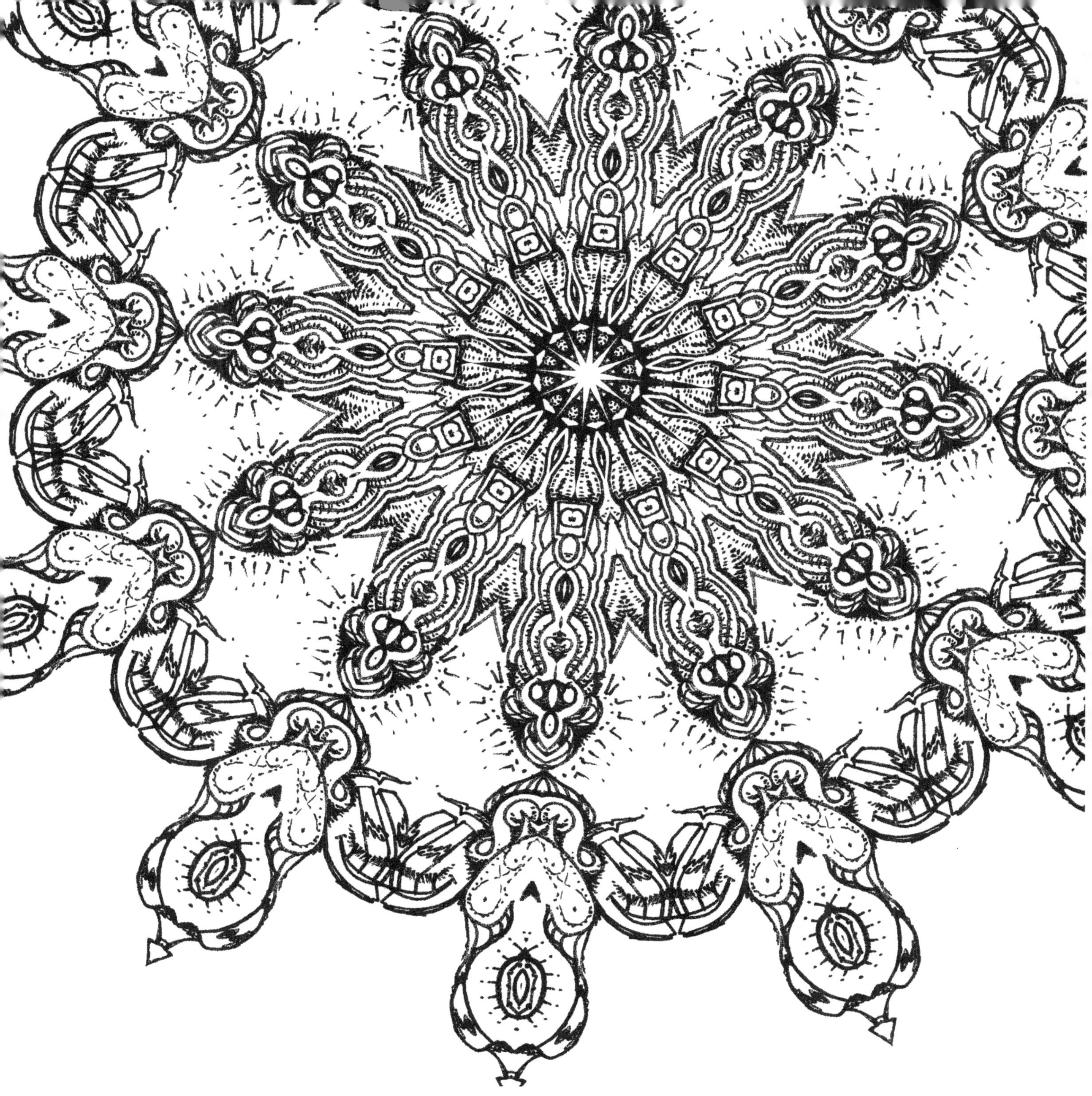

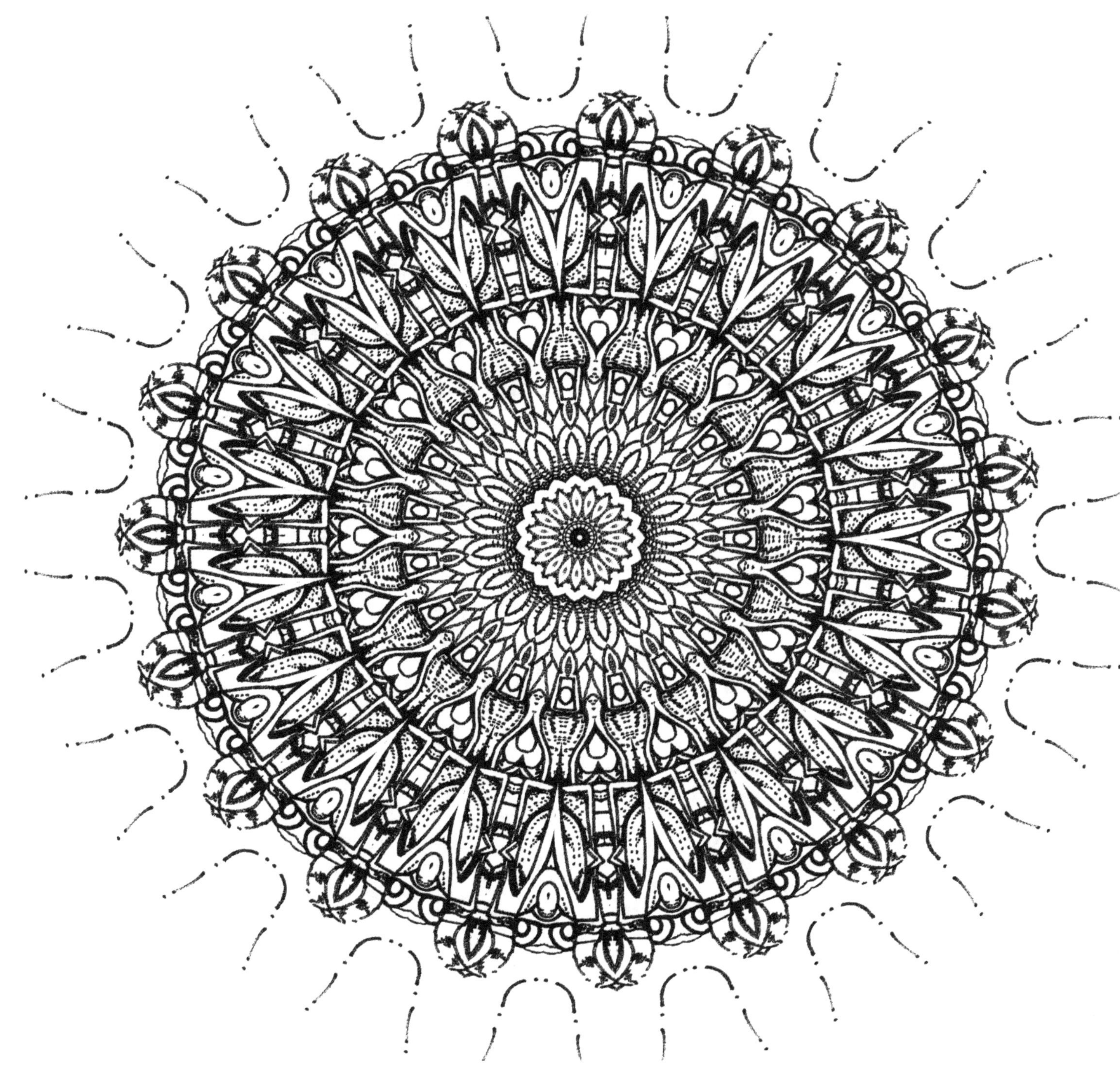

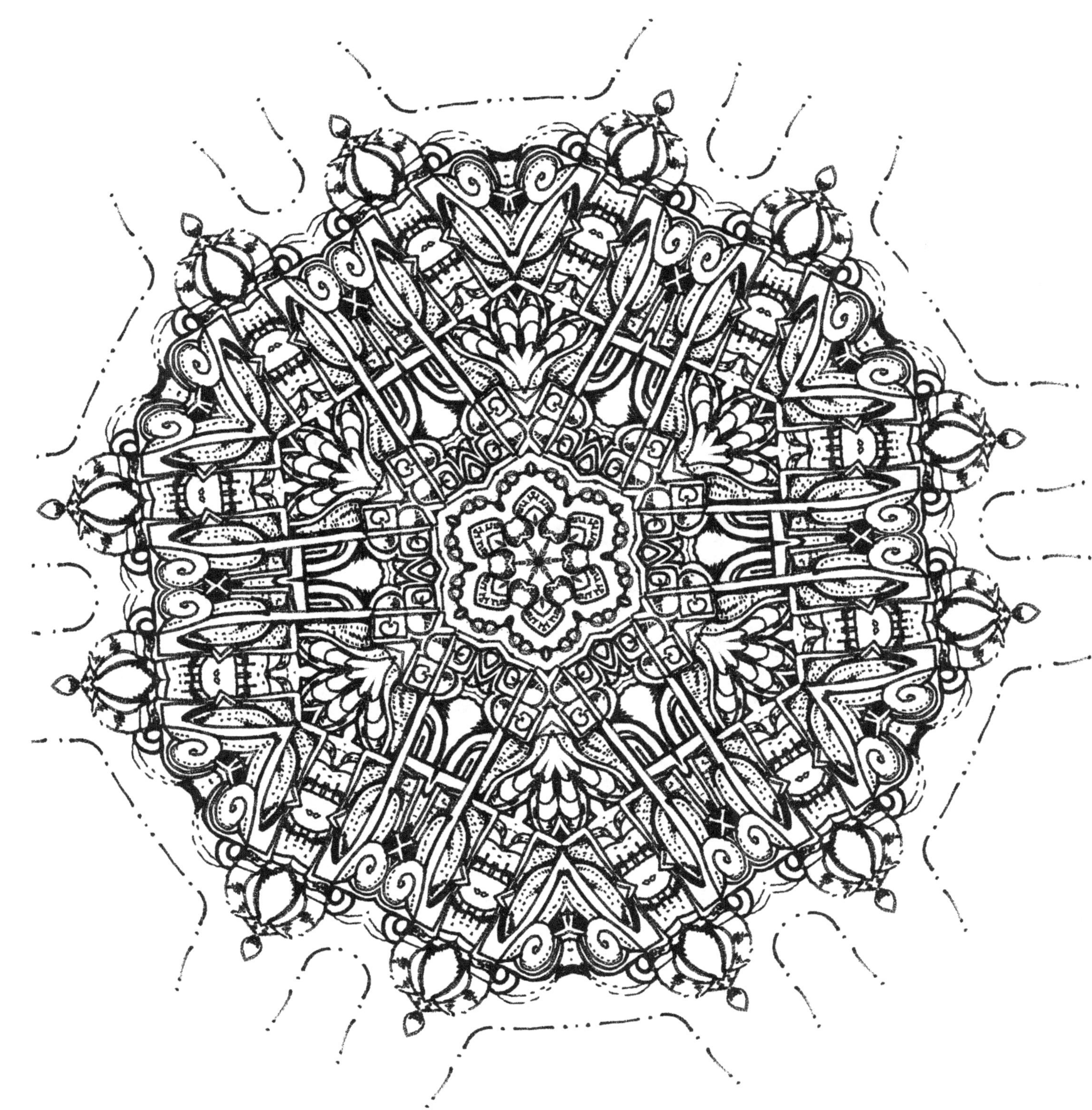

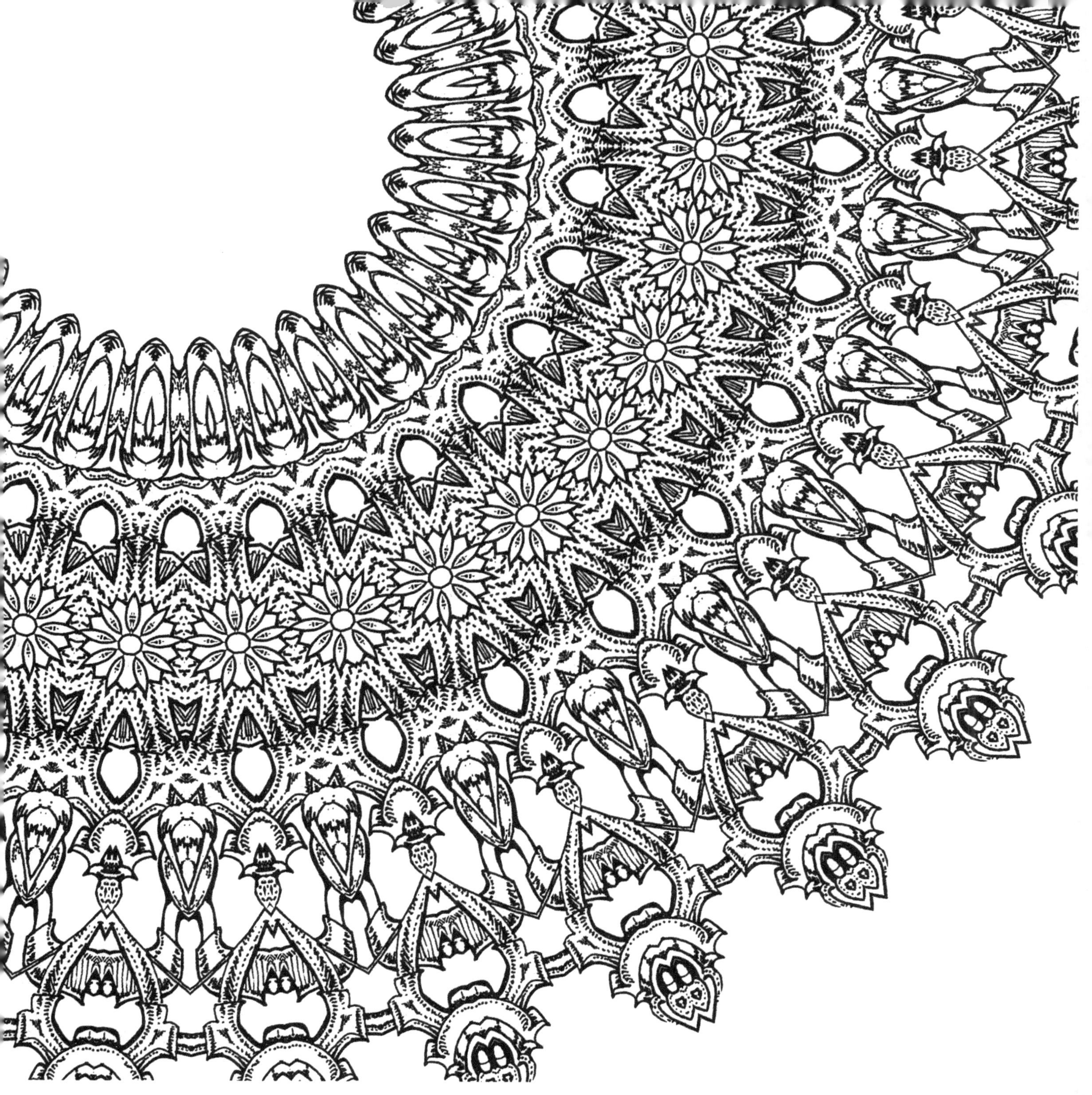